CIVICS
NOW

Authors

Doug Gordon

Jack MacFadden

Jennifer Watt

THOMSON

NELSON

Australia   Canada   Mexico   Singapore   Spain   United Kingdom   United States

THOMSON

NELSON

Civics Now
by Doug Gordon, Jack MacFadden, Jennifer Watt

Director of Publishing
Beverley Buxton

General Manager
Carol Stokes

Publisher
Doug Panasis

Managing Editor, Development
Leah-Ann Lymer

Assistant Editor
Alisa Yampolsky

Managing Editor, Production
Karin Fediw

Senior Production Coordinator
Kathrine Pummell

Design Director
Ken Phipps

Interior Design
Kyle Gell Design

Cover Design
Thomson Nelson Media Services

Printer
Transcontinental Printing Inc.

Focus Strategic Communications Inc.

Project Manager
Adrianna Edwards

Developmental Editors
Ron Edwards, Adrianna Edwards

Copyeditor
Jennie Worden

Proofreader
Linda Szostak

Index
Ron Edwards

Compositor
Lisa Platt

Photo Research and Permissions
Elizabeth Kelly

Dedications
To the memory of my parents, Geoff and Eileen, and father-in-law, Felix.

—Doug Gordon

To my wife and best friend, Josie. To my sons, Phillip, Johnny, and Daniel, thanks for your support. For my Dad, Jack MacFadden Sr., this book is for you!

—Jack MacFadden

This book is for Emma, with all my love—Mommy.

—Jennifer Watt

Reviewers
Brent Birchard
Durham District School Board

Gillian Bracking
Peel District School Board

Julia Cale
Huron-Perth Catholic District School Board

Roma Francis
De La Salle College "Oaklands"

Ivan Ius
Wellington Catholic District School Board

Alexandra Kucharczyk
Toronto Catholic District School Board

Doug McMillan
Toronto District School Board

Julie Neeb
Waterloo Region District School Board

Rachel M. Powell
Toronto District School Board

Aboriginal Content Reviewers
Brenda Davis
Six Nations

Rocky Landon
Limestone District School Board

Contents

UNIT 3: THE ACTIVE CITIZEN · 78

UNIT 4: THE GLOBAL CITIZEN · 134

Using *Civics Now*

Before Reading

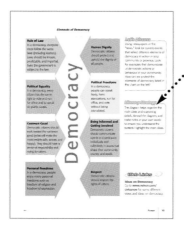

Literacy Strategy

These margin notes provide tools to help you better understand what you've read, manage and discuss the content, and apply the information to other situations. Use these strategies to help you plan your reading, organize your thoughts and ideas as you read, and reflect on what you've read once you have finished.

Unit Opener

Each unit opens with a large photograph that represents the unit. This is followed by a list of **Focus Questions** that contain the "big ideas" of the unit. The Focus Questions are repeated throughout the unit when a major topic is introduced.

Use the Focus Questions to access your prior knowledge or to guide you as you read. You can also use them to focus your note-taking and discussions, and review your understanding of the unit.

What Is This Unit About?

This summary of the unit prepares you for reading, and outlines the main ideas in the unit. Use this section to skim and preview the content. As you skim this summary, think about what you already know about the topic. You might create a web or a list to help you organize your thoughts before you begin reading. You can also return to this summary after reading, to review what you've covered in the unit.

During Reading

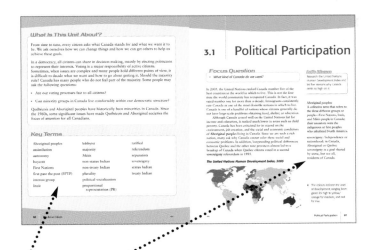

Key Terms

These are the new words that you need to know. They are defined in the margins the first time they are mentioned, unless they are explained in the text. They also are defined in the **Glossary** at the back of your textbook.

Preview the Key Terms before you begin reading, and look for their meaning in context as you read. If the meaning of the word is unclear, think of a word that looks similar, such as a word that has the same root. You can also return to these definitions as a quick content review.

Let's Discuss

These questions help you to preview the content before you read a passage, they guide you as you read, and they help you plan your tasks after you have finished reading.

Before you begin, read these questions to help you focus on the main ideas. As you read the passage, look for the answers, and jot them down. These questions may also contain tasks you are expected to perform when you're finished. Once you've read the passage, pause and reflect on what you've read. Make notes on the content and jot down your opinions and conclusions.

After Reading

Web Links

This margin note sends you to the Nelson *Civics Now* Web site to learn more about the people, places, and events discussed in your textbook.

Civics Now DVD

This margin note sends you to the Nelson *Civics Now* DVD, which contains video clips that bring the ideas in your textbook to life. While viewing the DVD, take note of how some of the concepts you have studied are applied in Canada.

Making a Difference

This feature introduces you to Canadians who have made a difference in their community, in Canada, or in the world. After you have finished reading a section or a unit, take time to reflect on a topic and determine how you could make a difference.

Civics Showcase

This feature helps you make connections between a civics topic and your own life.

Speaking Out!

This feature presents two or more viewpoints on an issue. Read the opinions, and decide what you believe and why. As you read, summarize the content, including your opinions. Use your notes to explain and justify your beliefs.

Ecohabits

This feature highlights actions we can take to improve our environment and our planet. Think about the task as you read, and jot down any ideas you may have prior to discussing them in your group.

Check Your Understanding

These questions provide a guide for you to summarize the content at the end of each section. Read the questions and answer them carefully, referring to the notes that you have made. If you're not sure of the answers, reread the section and jot down the main ideas in your own words. Then return to these questions to complete the answers.

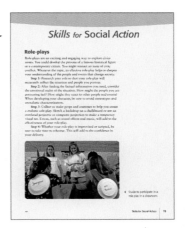

Skills for Social Action

This feature shows you how to develop an important skill. The skills include getting reliable information, coming up with the right questions on a civics topic, thinking about different viewpoints, interviewing people, and writing and presenting information. Plan the tasks ahead of time, and use the strategies that best suit you to help you perfect each skill.

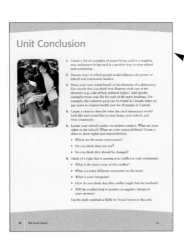

Unit Conclusion

Each unit ends with questions and activities that give you a chance to show what you've learned in the entire unit. Use your notes and your summarizing and reflecting strategies to help you reinforce your learning.

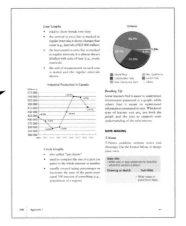

Appendix (Reading to Learn and Learning How to Learn)

The Appendix is designed to help you better understand content and apply skills. **Reading to Learn** provides step-by-step literacy strategies to help you learn how to read the content. **Learning How to Learn** provides ideas to help you learn content and apply skills.

The Good Citizen

Focus Questions

This unit explores these questions:

- *Why am I taking a civics course?*

- *How are decisions made in your society?*

- *Power—is it good or bad?*

- *How will your wants and needs be met?*

- *How do you settle arguments?*

- *What do you gain from democratic decision making?*

- *How do you define a responsible citizen?*

What Is This Unit About?

In a democracy, people are free to make choices.

- We choose our political leaders who make laws and policies to protect our freedoms.

- We try to respect all citizens, whatever their country of origin, their spoken language, and their religious beliefs.

- We try to balance the rights of the minority—whether French-speaking Québécois people, or Aboriginal people, or immigrant Canadians—with the rights of the majority.

- We attempt to maintain equality before the law.

- We try to provide equal access to health care and support for the elderly and those living in poverty.

Citizens need to be informed, be active, and have a sense of purpose. Democracy is complex. There are many issues and opinions to consider before and after decisions are made. A good citizen becomes actively involved in society. Will you?

Key Terms

arbitration

autocracy

autocratic decision making

basic needs

bias

common good

conciliation

consensual/collaborative decision making

consensus

consensus building

democracy

democratic decision making

discrimination

human dignity

inequalities

mediation

negotiation

power

psychological needs

society

wants

1.1 | What Is Civics?

- *Why am I taking a civics course?*

A course on civics involves the study of government, democratic decision making, and what it means to be an informed, active, and responsible citizen in local, national, and global contexts. In this course, you will learn how decisions get made, such as how much money is spent on the environment or how much money goes toward sports programs in your community. You will also learn how you can be involved in decisions that affect the society you live in.

Let's Discuss

What are your opinions about a civics course? On what information do you base your opinions (personal interest/ experience, views of friends)? What questions do you have about the civics course in general?

I'm not sure what to expect in this course. I like the idea that, during civics class, I will be learning more about politics and how I can make a difference in Canadian society.

I'm already really involved in my community. I watch the news almost every day, and I like debating political issues, especially about human rights. I hope to pursue a career having to do with politics or human rights.

I don't care about corrupt politicians or what's going on in the community. I just want to get a good job and make money for me and my family.

Why Does the Provincial Government Make Civics a Compulsory Course?

Let's Discuss

How involved are you in your community? Give examples. Discuss what you would like to do or change in your community.

▲ A young person enjoys skateboarding at a new sports centre.

1. Be a Better Citizen

An understanding of civics is intended to make you a better citizen, one who tries to make informed decisions and who wants to participate effectively in the community, nation, and world. A civics course will help you to develop the skills and attitudes that citizens living in a democracy need. These skills include looking at questions from several points of view; getting involved in issues of community, national, and global concern; and understanding and caring about the rights and freedoms of all people, not just your own.

2. Learn About Your Rights and Responsibilities

Many young people want to know more about their rights and responsibilities. They want to understand how government works in a democratic society, and how they can try to change things for the better. For example, a group of teenagers may think that their community should have a new sports centre. If they understand civics, they would know who to ask about the sports centre as well as how to get other people in the community to support their idea. They would recognize and appreciate that there are many other competing interests besides their own (having the roads paved, or getting a larger park, or building a daycare facility).

3. Learn About Canadian Government and Politics

A civics course will help you discover more about government and will give you a basic understanding of how democracy functions and how you can change things. Canada needs citizens who understand how government works at all levels, who participate actively in their communities, and who contribute their knowledge and skills to make Canadian society better for all its citizens.

By the end of this course, you will be able to define what makes a good citizen—in your classroom, school, community, country, and the world. You will be able to say what being a citizen means to you. You will discover that citizenship gives you many rights. Along with these rights, though, come responsibilities. You will discover what these rights and responsibilities are.

1.2 | Your Classroom: A Society in Miniature

Focus Question

- *How are decisions made in your society?*

As you sit in a group in your class, take a minute to consider the following questions with a cooperative group:

- What are your goals in this course?

- Who will ensure that these goals are met?

- How do we ensure that most goals are met?

Write your answers on chart paper. Compare your answers with those of other groups, and discuss the following questions:

- What goals were shared by all the groups?

- What goals were different?

- Were the goals realistic?

- What rules would have to be agreed on if these goals were to be achieved?

Literacy Strategy

Before reading, skim and preview the content of this section. Note how the questions help you organize your thoughts and guide your reading.

Let's Discuss

As a whole class, select five main goals from all the ideas that have been presented. How will you decide which goals are most important? Why did you choose a certain method to come to a decision? What factors influenced your decision?

Making Decisions

If you chose to vote, with the majority vote making the decision, your class is modelling one type of **democracy**. Define **democratic decision making** in your own words.

democratic decision making: A process by which a group decision is made by a majority vote.

autocratic decision making: A process by which one person makes a decision for a group.

consensual/collaborative decision making: A process by which everyone in the group must agree before a decision is made.

If one person (e.g., the teacher) or a small group of people has been given the power to decide, your class is modelling an **autocracy**. Define **autocratic decision making** in your own words.

If you try to reach a **consensus** (everyone must be in agreement) for the decision, your class is working collaboratively. In other words, everyone must work together to reach a decision and agree with that decision. Define, in your own words, **consensual/collaborative decision making.** In your own experience, what are some of the things that get in the way in consensual/collaborative decision making?

↔ Check Your Understanding

1. Consider the following scenarios:
   - A family is trying to decide how household duties will be shared.
   - A basketball team must decide who will be the starting players for the game.
   - A class is trying to choose one activity for fundraising.
   - A group of friends is deciding what movie or club to go to.
   - The principal is asking for input on what to do to prevent locker break-ins.

   a) Which form of decision making would you suggest for each scenario? Give reasons for your answer.

   b) Complete the chart on the right in your notes. Choose two of the above scenarios. Consider the pros and cons of these three ways of making decisions for each scenario you have chosen. Include points that interest you about sharing power.

Democratic decision making	Autocratic decision making	Consensual/collaborative decision making

2. For this entire exercise, you have been working as a "citizen" of your classroom. Which of the following qualities do you think are the most important for a classroom citizen? Rank the three qualities that, in your view, are the most important and the three qualities that are the least important. Are there other important qualities that are missing from this list?

   - comes on time
   - is friendly with all students
   - participates actively
   - helps group members to achieve their best
   - gets high marks

   - respects the teacher
   - respects other students
   - reports someone cheating on a major test
   - shares relevant personal experiences during discussions

   - runs for student council
   - helps keep the classroom clean
   - comes to the aid of a teacher or student who is being verbally threatened

1.3 Power

Focus Question

- *Power—is it good or bad?*

In any group of people—whether it is your classroom, your sports team, or your circle of friends—some people have more **power** than others. One definition of power is the ability to achieve what you want. Within a group, power can be defined as the ability to get others to do what you want. There are many reasons why one person is more powerful than others. These include greater intelligence, persuasiveness, charisma, money, physical strength, attractiveness, and social status.

Power is a natural part of being human. We use it every day. We can use power to achieve personal and shared goals. We can also use power to deny certain people or groups equal opportunities to meet their needs and wants. This misuse of power can lead to **discrimination** and **inequalities**. Power can be very destructive in the wrong hands, but it can also be constructive if it is used to promote equality and improve lives.

power: The ability of an individual or group to get what it wants.

discrimination: The unfavourable or prejudiced treatment of an individual or group based on race, sex, appearance, income, and so on.

inequalities: A term often used to refer to the differences in our society where some people have more money, education, and other resources than other people; these differences may be the result of discrimination.

Literacy Strategy

During reading, pause and think about what you're reading. Using what you already know about power, try to make connections between the text passage and the world you live in.

▲ A student assists a senior at a local seniors' centre.

Types of Power

There are many types of power that operate within our society and in the larger global community. Military power can be used for both good and evil ends. Political power and influence can be used positively or negatively. Corporate power can be used to benefit consumers and employees or to promote greed and overcharging. In a democracy, the voters and consumers ultimately judge how well elected leaders and large corporations use their power to satisfy the voter and the buyer.

Influence

People are constantly trying to influence politicians to do certain things. Interest groups will exert influence on decision makers— sometimes for the public interest, sometimes for private gain. If power is used responsibly, most people in a democratic society will benefit.

↔ Check Your Understanding

Consider the following scenarios. Write briefly how power is used in five of these scenarios. In which scenarios is power being used in a forceful way? In which scenarios is power being used in a persuasive way? In which scenarios is power based on rewards?

1. A mother insists that her children go to bed by 8:00 P.M. or they will lose their television privileges.

2. A student persuades the class to stop buying hamburgers at a certain restaurant because the extra packaging used by the restaurant is harming the environment.

3. You know that if you speak out against the government leader, you will "disappear."

4. You purchase a brand of running shoes that is endorsed by a major sports figure.

5. After watching pre-election TV ads for several weeks, you vote for a political party.

6. Your parents give you extra money for the "A's" on your report card.

7. After an earthquake, looters are imprisoned without trial.

▲ A soldier hands out food to children. Is this an example of positive or negative power?

Are Humans Good or Evil?

Thomas Hobbes, a famous British philosopher in the 1600s, felt that all people are born selfish and will seek only their own interests. This selfishness often leads to violence and war. Hobbes thought people should be taught obedience, enforced by a supreme ruler, in order to avoid chaos.

A hundred years later, French philosopher Jean-Jacques Rousseau disagreed with Hobbes's ideas and argued instead that the natural state of humans was one of peace and harmony. He saw democracy as a reflection of our basic sense of fairness and equality.

Questions

1. Do you agree with Hobbes or Rousseau?

2. List three things you see in your life and in society that support either Hobbes or Rousseau. Discuss the photographs below as part of your evidence.

▲ Clockwise from top left: Volunteers help in a food drive. Students get involved in recycling. Young people help out in a soup kitchen. Soldiers fight in a military conflict.

Society: The Bigger Picture

Focus Question

- *How will your wants and needs be met?*

A **society** is a community of people who share **basic needs** and **wants**. Some of the most basic needs of a community are food and water and clothing and shelter. "Wants" are those things that are not essential for survival, but people desire and value them anyway. Cell phones, vacations, and multiple pairs of jeans are examples of individual wants. Life today is complex, and we have many wants and needs. Besides basic needs, there are also **psychological needs**. People need to feel safe, secure, and happy in their community.

It is not easy for societies to work out how to meet the basic needs and wants of their citizens. How will a society balance the shared needs of its citizens with what certain individual people or groups want? How do we decide what is fair?

True Democracy

Every society has a variety of groups with different wants and needs. In a democracy, all citizens have a voice in the decision making. Decisions reflect the will of the majority. Members of a democratic society live in freedom. The government is limited in its power and must respect people's rights.

Citizens in a democracy not only enjoy their rights and freedoms, but they must also take very seriously the responsibilities of living democratically. They should uphold **human dignity**, respect the rights of others, work for the **common good**, and have a sense of responsibility for other people. Taking part in public discussion and debate on civic issues is another important responsibility of the democratic citizen.

The Enemies of Democracy

In all communities, there will be some people who don't care about their responsibilities as citizens. They don't understand how democracy works or why it is important to their lives. Other people may decide not to get involved in many aspects of democratic citizenship.

Let's Discuss

One need of modern society is schools to educate young people. List at least ten other examples of needs in a modern society.

basic needs: Things people need for physical survival, such as food, shelter, and clothing.

wants: Goods or services that people desire but that are not necessary for survival.

psychological needs: Things people need for emotional reasons, such as safety and security.

human dignity: The feeling that one is respected and valued in a society.

common good: What will make the most people safe, secure, and happy.

Web Links

Information on Democracy
For current new articles and information on Canadian democracy, social justice, and environmental and health issues, go to **www.nelson.com/civicsnow.**

This girl is an active participant in her community recycling program.

Enemies of Democracy

"In the election for student council president, I'll just vote for the first name I recognize. I don't have time to get into the issues."

"My family already pays taxes for garbage collection. Why should I bother with recycling?"

"My family and I come first. We have our own set of beliefs, and we don't need the government to make laws telling us what is right and wrong."

"Those people are always protesting something. The police should just arrest them."

Questions

1. Above are some examples of actions and beliefs that could be harmful in a democracy. Explain why these actions and beliefs could have a negative impact on the way democracy works in your community.

2. What arguments might you use to convince the person to change his or her views?

Clothing With Conscience

Being a good local, national, and global citizen involves taking care of the environment. Besides recycling, there are countless ways that you can become a citizen who cares for the environment, such as ecologically friendly habits involving clothing.

- Buy your clothes at a secondhand clothing store. Swap or alternate clothes with your friends instead of buying new.

- Buy clothes that are made from organic cotton or hemp. Organic cotton is grown without the use of pesticides. Hemp is a naturally pest-resistant crop that requires less water to grow than cotton does. Look for manufacturers that use environmentally friendly products and methods.

- Dry cleaning fluid is toxic to people and the environment. Buy clothes that can be washed, or look for dry cleaners that do not use perchloroethylene (Perc).

- Wash your clothes in cold water.

Questions

1. Visit your local dry cleaner, and find out if they use Perc. If so, ask about other ways of cleaning your clothes, or find a dry cleaner that does not use Perc. Report your findings to your class.

2. Research three or four manufacturers that use environmentally friendly products and methods. Share this with your class.

3. List environmentally friendly options for other products.

▲ A teen shops at a local secondhand clothing store.

Elements of Democracy

Rule of Law
In a democracy, everyone must follow the same laws (including leaders). Laws should be known, predictable, and impartial. Even the government is subject to the law.

Political Equality
In a democracy, every citizen has the same right to vote and run for office and to speak on public issues.

Common Good
Democratic citizens should work toward the common good (what will make the most people safe, secure, and happy). They should have a sense of responsibility and caring for others.

Personal Freedoms
In a democracy, people enjoy many personal freedoms such as freedom of religion and freedom of expression.

Democracy

Human Dignity
Democratic citizens should protect and uphold the dignity of all people.

Political Freedoms
In a democracy, people can speak freely, form associations, run for office, and vote without being intimidated.

Being Informed and Getting Involved
Democratic citizens should communicate openly and participate individually and collectively in issues that shape their community, country, and world.

Respect
Democratic citizens should respect the rights of others.

Let's Discuss

Using newspapers or the "news," look for current events that reflect different elements of democracy in action in your community or province. Look for examples that demonstrate undemocratic actions or behaviour in your community. How can we protect the elements of democracy listed in the chart on the left?

Literacy Strategy

The diagram helps organize the main ideas and supporting details. Reread the diagram, and make notes in your own words to ensure you understand the content. Highlight the main ideas.

Web Links

Ideas on Democracy
Go to **www.nelson.com/ civicsnow** for some different views and ideas on democracy.

Conflict Resolution

Focus Question

- *How do you settle arguments?*

consensus building:
A process by which a group makes a decision only when everyone is in agreement.

Literacy Strategy

Before reading, skim and preview the heading, the Focus Question, and the photo. Predict the content of this page. Think about how you would settle an argument before reading, and jot down your ideas. After reading, make a connection between your solution and the terms found on this page.

People often disagree about what they want or need. These disagreements can lead to arguments and conflicts, which can be resolved either physically or verbally. Physical solutions generally involve violence such as fighting or war. Often, the problem can be solved through discussion, verbal persuasion, or **consensus building**.

These are some ways to resolve conflicts verbally:

- **Negotiation**—Both parties discuss the issues and try to resolve differences, being careful to avoid negative, blaming language. Usually both parties have to give up some of their demands in order to reach a compromise.

- **Mediation**—A third party helps both parties arrive at a solution to the conflict.

- **Arbitration**—A third party is given the power to decide the outcome of the conflict.

- **Conciliation**—A third party clearly defines both the points of agreement and the points of difference that must be resolved to end the conflict.

At school, students are sometimes involved in negotiating conflicts. Many schools have trained student mediators to help peers settle issues. Only as a last resort does the teacher or vice principal step in as an authority figure. In society at large, some situations require similar methods. In a labour dispute, both parties may try to negotiate a solution. If unsuccessful, they may request a mediator or an arbitrator to settle their differences. Citizens also depend on government, police, and the court system to resolve conflicts.

◀ Students resolve a conflict by talking about it with each other.

1.4 Democratic Decision Making

- *What do you gain from democratic decision making?*

Before reading, skim and preview, and ask yourself questions about what you are about to read. Find the answers in this text passage.

In every society, individuals and groups have different views about how their needs should be met. It is a natural result of people living together in groups. The types of social conflict can range from lively discussion and debate to violent action.

One way of solving civic conflict is through democratic decision making. It is important because it values all people equally. Everyone is entitled to a say, either directly or through an elected representative. No one voice is more important than another. The rights of all citizens are respected equally.

Democratic decision making can succeed only if people have the skills and attitudes to work together to resolve conflict. Two of the main skills needed for a successful democracy are the effective expressing of ideas, as well as listening to and carefully considering the ideas of others. Democratic decision making skills should be learned and the art of compromise practised to be effective. Otherwise, individuals will demand that only their own needs be met without considering the needs of others.

Here are the basic principles of democratic decision making:

1. Each person has something positive to offer, and each person has something positive to gain.

2. Each person must be accountable for his or her actions.

3. Each person in a group must participate in some equal way.

4. There must be a method for reaching the decision.

5. A decision must be made.

▲ A woman voices her opinion on the use of old-growth trees for the timber industry with a colourful sign.

Difference

Rosemary Brown

Democratic decision making was one of the central factors in Rosemary Brown's life. Politician, teacher, and social worker, she was a leading African–Canadian pioneer who fought for equality for all Canadians. Her work helped to pass a new *Human Rights Code* so that everyone would be treated fairly.

Rosemary Brown was the first Black woman ever elected to a provincial legislature in Canada. She was also the first woman to run for the leadership of a federal political party—the New Democratic Party. That was in 1975, and although she did not win the leadership, it was still a milestone for racial and female advancement. In 1996, she was named Officer of the Order of Canada for her work on human rights.

Questions

1. Why is Rosemary Brown a good example of an informed, active, and purposeful citizen?

2. Name three other Canadians you think deserve to be appointed to the Order of Canada. Be prepared to defend your choices.

▲ Governor General Roméo LeBlanc congratulates Rosemary Brown after she receives the Order of Canada.

Literacy Strategy

After you read, reflect on how you might make a connection between the content and the world you live in. Be prepared to state your opinions, draw conclusions, and make judgments. Can you justify your thinking?

1.5 | The Responsible Citizen

Focus Question

- *How do you define a responsible citizen?*

So far, we have examined a few ways in which decisions can be made in a society and discussed civic conflict. What is the role of the citizen in society? Who exactly is a citizen? A dictionary definition states that a citizen is an inhabitant of a city or country. There are, however, many sides to the meaning of citizenship. How we define "citizen" depends on our point of view.

↔ Check Your Understanding

Examine the viewpoints on the right that illustrate some of the many meanings of citizenship.

1. Why are there so many variations of the term "citizen"?

2. What are the qualities of a "responsible" citizen in terms of what that person knows, does, or thinks?

3. Assess the people on the right in terms of the qualities you have developed. What additional questions would you ask them?

4. What do you think has influenced their definition of citizen?

5. Write a quotation that summarizes your definition of a citizen.

"I was born here. I'm a Canadian citizen."

"I devote my time and energies to helping homeless people. Politics seems not as important as these real-life problems that I can help solve directly."

"My supreme leader is God. I follow religious leaders and laws, not secular ones."

"My responsibility is to the world as a whole. I live in Canada, but I care about environmental issues worldwide. Every person must be responsible for caring for our world."

"This is a great country. We have a democratic government, freedom, a high standard of living, good health care, and great natural beauty. I'm proud to be a Canadian."

"I'm interested in what is happening back in my homeland. I became a citizen of Canada for better opportunities for my family and me."

"I am Cree. We had a nation long before Canada existed as one."

Skills *for* Social *Action*

Locating and Evaluating Sources

Television

Television has both great strengths and great weaknesses as a source of information. Visual images have a powerful emotional impact—some viewers believe the camera does not lie. Television newscasts are limited sources of information. The average half-hour television newscast contains the same amount of information as half a newspaper page. So, start your investigation with television, but don't stop there.

The Internet

The Internet is an enormous resource of information, but all Web sites are not created equal. Ask yourself: Who is behind the content of a particular site, and how reliable is the information? Does the Web site reflect the views of an individual person or a group? Does it contain unfair and biased perspectives on an issue?

Internet sites can be created and run by just about anyone. For example, television networks, newspapers, and government and educational Web sites often have valuable information on civics topics. Individual Web logs can provide different viewpoints on many issues that are often ignored by mainstream news. Always use other sources in addition to Internet sites to complement your research.

Newspapers

Newspapers are a rich source of information that can supplement what you learned from a television news story or a Web site. In newspaper stories, the headline and first few sentences convey the most important facts about the story in order to capture our interest immediately. The secondary details, which are revealed as the story unfolds, are important for a student researching a topic. Many published newspapers are available online, as are independent news agencies that publish only electronically.

Community Resources

Community resources are available on certain topics. Local, provincial, and national governments often have information on particular topics on their Web sites or in printed reports. Speaking with local officials, government departments, or people active in their community can be arranged.

Determining the Reliability of Sources

Suppose you are interested in the possible closing of a school in your community and attend a school board meeting where the issue is discussed. How would your account of the meeting compare with the coverage by television, the Internet, or the newspaper?

All four sources—television, the Internet, newspaper, and your own account—reflect a certain bias. **Bias** is the emphasizing of certain facts over others. You should attempt to assess the amount of bias that is present in all sources. Television is naturally biased in favour of a good visual story. Newspapers may be biased in the choice of headlines and lead paragraphs to grab readers' interest. Newspaper editorials have an obvious bias, called a point of view, and they are selective in the use of facts to support it.

By using as wide a variety of sources as possible, you can filter out the biases and obtain the information necessary to evaluate an issue in civics.

Unit Conclusion

1. Create a list of examples of power being used in a negative way and power being used in a positive way in your school and community.

2. Discuss ways in which people could influence the power of school and community leaders.

3. Draw your own visual based on the elements of a democracy. Use visuals that you think best illustrate each one of the elements (e.g., rule of law, political rights). Add specific examples from your life for each of the main headings. For example, the common good can be found in Canada when we pay taxes to support health care for all people in Canada.

4. Create a chart to describe what the ideal democracy would look like and sound like in your home, your school, and your community.

5. Locate your school's policy on student conduct. What are your rights in the school? What are your responsibilities? Create a chart to show rights and responsibilities.

   • Which are the most controversial?

   • Do you think these are fair?

   • Do you think they should be changed?

6. Think of a topic that is causing civic conflict in your community.

   • What is the main cause of this conflict?

   • What are some different viewpoints on the issue?

   • What is your viewpoint?

   • How do you think that this conflict might best be resolved?

   • Will the conflict lead to positive or negative change in your opinion?

   Use the skills outlined in Skills for Social Action in this unit.

7. Ongoing Collaborative Project

"The Good Citizen": An Interactive Bulletin Board

Create an interactive bulletin board in your classroom entitled "The Good Citizen." Include newspaper articles, drawings, photos, and quotations from songs, speeches, and movies. Make it a mix of pictures, words, phrases, poetry, comments, and art. Add contributions to the board display to show what you have learned about the issues of citizenship. Consider the board a work in progress; you and your teacher should feel free to add as many contributions as you want at any time. Don't forget to explain contributions to the class. You can create a Web page instead of a bulletin board.

The Informed Citizen

Focus Questions

This unit explores these questions:

- *How does a person become a Canadian citizen?*

- *What are your rights and responsibilities as a Canadian citizen?*

- *Why are your rights limited?*

- *How has democracy changed in Canada since 1867?*

- *How are candidates elected in Canada?*

- *How are federal and provincial governments organized in Canada?*

- *How do the federal and provincial governments make public policy?*

- *What are the powers and functions of the federal, provincial, and municipal governments?*

- *How do the federal and provincial governments make laws and regulations?*

- *What is the function of political parties in the Canadian system?*

- *What are the roles and responsibilities of the courts?*

- *How does the judicial system protect the rights of individuals and society?*

What Is This Unit About?

The "Informed Citizen" takes responsibility for participating in the decision making process by

- voting

- being aware of current issues of government policy

- understanding how government organizations operate

- becoming involved in the democratic process

- actively working on political and social issues

When we fail to take responsibility and inform ourselves as citizens, we weaken our ability to participate in democracy. We create a weaker society and let other people decide how we will live.

Key Terms

bill	franchise	political ideology
candidate	impartial	political parties
committee	legislation	popular vote
Constitution	legislature	riding
election	multicultural	Royal Commission
electoral district	nomination	Speech from the Throne

2.1 | Citizenship Rights and Responsibilities

Focus Question

• *How does a person become a Canadian citizen?*

Today's Canadians come from many parts of the world. If you walk through a shopping mall or take a bus in a major Canadian city, you see people of different colours and races. Modern Canada is a **multicultural** society, but to be a Canadian is not to be a particular race, colour, or religion. To be a Canadian citizen means to share in a particular set of values and obligations that comes from living in our democracy.

Each year, thousands of people immigrate to this country. They do this for many reasons. Some come because they believe that Canada will provide new opportunities for themselves and their families. Others come to avoid political persecution in their own lands. New Canadians contribute to our society in many ways as they work hard to build a new life. Most new immigrants become citizens and then are able to share with Canadians born in Canada all the rights and responsibilities that citizenship brings.

multicultural: A description of a nation, such as Canada, that allows many different ethnic groups to retain their own languages, religions, and cultures with tolerance and without discrimination.

▶ Canadians of all backgrounds enjoy the rights and responsibilities of Canadian citizenship.

From Immigrant to Citizen

Literacy Strategy

Skim the heading, photos, and margin notes. Predict the content of this page. Think about what you already know about the topic before you begin to read. Use your prior knowledge to help you better understand the text.

Many new immigrants to Canada become Canadian citizens. There are three ways to become a Canadian citizen:

1. People born in Canada are automatically Canadian citizens.

2. People born outside Canada after February 15, 1977, and who have one Canadian parent are citizens.

3. Immigrants to Canada from other countries do not automatically become Canadian citizens. Usually, new immigrants are classed as permanent residents, with some of the rights of Canadian citizens. In order for a newcomer to Canada to become a Canadian citizen, he or she must meet certain requirements. The federal government lists the following:

   • be at least 18 years of age

   • have been a permanent resident of Canada for three years

   • have knowledge of Canada, including the rights and responsibilities of citizenship

   • be able to speak either English or French, the two official languages of Canada

About 150 000 immigrants become Canadian citizens every year. They must take a test in one of the two official languages, which covers many aspects of Canadian life, history, and geography, including the voting process, and the rights and responsibilities of citizenship. In fact, new citizens must know many of the same things that you will learn in this course.

▲ A group of immigrants participate in a swearing-in ceremony to become new Canadian citizens.

Speaking Out!

Immigrants in Canada

"There are too many immigrants coming to Canada. We don't have enough jobs for the people who already live here. Canada has really changed over the past 30 years. My kids can't get jobs because ethnic minorities get them all."

"I think new immigrants have made Canada a very exciting place to live. Canada used to be so stuffy and uptight. I love visiting neighbourhoods in my city that reflect a different background. I like to go and try all the different foods in a variety of restaurants. From what I've seen, most new immigrants work very hard. It must be very tough to come to a new country and start all over again. They deserve our admiration."

Questions

1. In your own words, describe what each speaker believes about immigration.

2. Make a list of experiences that may have led the speakers to make these comments.

3. Are there students in your school who have recently immigrated to Canada? What does your school do to help them adjust to life in Canada? How can you help them?

Web Links

Citizenship and Immigration
To learn more about citizenship and immigration and to review the actual application forms for Canadian citizenship, go to **www.nelson.com/civicsnow.**

Civics Now DVD

"Chinese Boat People" from *Civics Now DVD*.

▲ New immigrants to Canada have changed the faces of many neighbourhoods, such as this Chinatown in Toronto.

Pier 21: The Symbol of a New Life for Immigrants Coming to Canada

From 1928 to 1971, Pier 21, on the docks of Halifax, had been the key destination for most new immigrants to Canada. During the 1940s and 1950s, 3800 immigrants a day arrived through this huge barn-like building. After it was closed in 1971, Pier 21 became a historic site.

On July 1, 1999, the Pier 21 Historical Museum was officially opened by Justice Rosalie Abella of the Supreme Court of Canada. The Abella family immigrated in 1950 and entered Canada through Pier 21.

Question

Find a family member, friend, or neighbour who immigrated to Canada. Interview him or her about his or her experiences and share with a classmate. Have the class discuss what kinds of questions to ask during the interview.

▲ (left) Today, Pier 21 is a museum of Canadian immigration. (right) From 1928 to 1971, Pier 21 was the main gateway for most immigrants to Canada.

The Constitution

Constitution: The body of rules or laws by which Canada is governed; passed in 1982, it contains Canada's new *Charter of Rights and Freedoms*, the amending formula, and the 1867 *British North America Act*.

The rights of Canadian citizenship are defined in law and outlined in the Canadian **Constitution**. Canada's Constitution describes the basic principles that govern Canada. The Canadian Constitution is a combination of written and unwritten. So, in some ways, it resembles the American Constitution, which is mostly written down. In other ways, it is like the British Constitution, which is largely unwritten.

The Parts of Canada's Constitution

The written part of Canada's Constitution is outlined in the *Canada Act*, 1982. This includes

- the *Constitution Act*, 1867 (formerly known as the *British North America Act*, 1867)

- all amendments to the *British North America Act*, 1867

- the acts bringing British Columbia, Manitoba, Prince Edward Island, Alberta, Saskatchewan, and Newfoundland into Confederation

- the *Statute of Westminster*, 1931

- the *Constitution Act*, 1982; Part 1: *Canadian Charter of Rights and Freedoms*

Bringing the Constitution Home

In 1982, Prime Minister Pierre Trudeau succeeded in bringing home from Britain the written parts of Canada's Constitution, as listed above. The power to amend, or change, the Constitution was transferred to Canada on April 17, 1982, after the federal government and all the provinces except Quebec agreed on an amending formula. The amending formula requires the consent of the federal Parliament and the **legislatures** of seven provinces that make up at least 50 percent of the population.

legislature: A body of people with the power to make laws.

▲ Queen Elizabeth II signs the *Canada Act* on April 17, 1982, as Prime Minister Trudeau (seated) looks on.

Web Links

The Canadian Constitution
For a complete set of all the documents that make up the Canadian Constitution and the lead-up documents, go to **www.nelson.com/civicsnow**. The collection includes documents for events such as the addition of Newfoundland and Labrador as a province.

Literacy Strategy

As you read, jot down the main ideas in a graphic organizer, such as a timeline. Add supporting details to each note. Later, use your graphic organizer to help you review the content of the section.

The *Canadian Charter of Rights and Freedoms*

Focus Question

- *What are your rights and responsibilities as a Canadian citizen?*

Web Links

The *Canadian Charter of Rights and Freedoms*

To learn more about the *Canadian Charter of Rights and Freedoms,* go to **www.nelson.com/civicsnow.**

The *Canadian Charter of Rights and Freedoms* came into effect in 1982 as part of the Canadian Constitution. It outlines the rights of Canadian citizens and permanent residents. These rights include

1. **Fundamental freedoms**
   - freedom of conscience and religion
   - freedom of thought, belief, opinion, and expression
   - freedom of peaceful assembly
   - freedom of association

2. **Mobility rights**
   - the right to live and work in any province or territory

3. **Legal rights**
   - the right to not be detained or imprisoned without good cause
   - the right to be informed promptly of the reasons for arrest
   - the right to a lawyer without delay, and to not be imprisoned without the existence of a crime (and to be released if the imprisonment cannot be justified in a reasonable amount of time)
   - the right to be presumed innocent until proven guilty
   - the right not to be subjected to cruel and unusual treatment or punishment

4. **Equality rights**
   - the right to equal treatment by the law and protection from discrimination on the basis of race, national or ethnic origin, colour, religion, age, sex, or mental or physical disability

Let's Discuss

The *Canadian Charter of Rights and Freedoms* gave the Supreme Court of Canada more power to overrule provincial and federal laws that violate the rights of Canadian citizens and groups. With your class, discuss a recent Supreme Court decision that has caused public outcry and the reasons for the controversy.

5. **Official languages of Canada**
    - the right to access the government of Canada in English or French

6. **Minority language educational rights**
    - the right to education in English or French where there are significant numbers of students

For Canadians Only

Certain important rights apply only to Canadian citizens, and not to permanent residents. These rights are

- to cast a vote in a federal or provincial **election**
- to be a **candidate** in a federal or provincial election
- to be able to leave the country and return, regardless of the time spent abroad

Limitations of Rights

Focus Question

- *Why are your rights limited?*

All rights have limitations, or are limited. For example, the *Charter* outlines the right to freedom of speech, but when individuals use their free speech to hurt others, such as by spreading hate literature, someone else's rights are affected. In these situations, courts may be required to decide whose rights have priority.

Governments try to make laws that meet the *Charter* requirements. This can be difficult because some of the sections of the *Charter* are not clear. For example, what exactly is a cruel and unusual punishment (see number 3, page 32)? What actions actually are discriminatory (see number 4, page 32)?

Organizations or individuals sometimes challenge laws or regulations on the grounds that they do not meet the *Charter* requirements. In these cases, the courts decide whether a law is acceptable—a power that has created considerable controversy. We will look at this in more detail on page 71.

election: A process by which citizens vote for their representatives in government from a list of candidates running for office.

candidate: A person who chooses to run in an election; often a person who has been chosen by a political party to run for office.

▲ A Royal Canadian Mounted Police (RCMP) officer searches a protester at the U.S./Canada border. Are the protestor' rights more important than public safety?

Citizenship Rights and Responsibilities   **33**

Difference

Pierre Elliott Trudeau

Pierre Elliott Trudeau served as prime minister for over 15 years, and is remembered for many achievements. These included bringing home from Britain the Constitution, in 1982, and the adoption of the *Canadian Charter of Rights and Freedoms*. Some Canadians believe his policies are responsible for today's constitutional difficulties. Others view him as one of Canada's greatest statesmen.

Question
Ask your parents or grandparents what they remember about Trudeau. Is their reaction positive or negative? Why?

▲ This is former Prime Minister Pierre Elliott Trudeau. One of his greatest achievements was the adoption of the *Canadian Charter of Rights and Freedoms.*

Literacy Strategy

After you have read the feature and done the assignment, make judgments about Trudeau as a leader and justify your conclusions.

The Bill of Rights

Prior to the adoption of the *Canadian Charter of Rights and Freedoms* in 1982, the *Canadian Bill of Rights* of 1960 recognized civil rights in Canadian law. This bill outlined the following rights:

1. freedom of religion

2. freedom of the press

3. freedom of speech

4. freedom of assembly and association

5. equality before the law

6. life, liberty, security of the person, and enjoyment of property

▲ People demonstrate at Queen's Park (the Ontario Legislature) for the rights of homeless people. The *Charter* guarantees our rights to protest peacefully.

The *Canadian Bill of Rights* was not perfect. It was not part of the Canadian Constitution, so it did not apply to provincial laws. Furthermore, because it was not part of the Constitution, it did not necessarily override other existing laws. Courts were hesitant to use the *Bill* to expand rights or override any laws. Although the purpose of the *Canadian Bill of Rights* was noble, its effectiveness was limited. However, many of its ideas were used in the *Charter*.

Human Rights

Provincial legislatures have also passed laws that outline fundamental rights. In fact, provincial legislatures passed human rights **legislation** before the federal government did. For example, Saskatchewan had a *Bill of Rights* in 1947.

In Ontario, the *Human Rights Code* defines some of the specific rights of Ontario residents. These rights include freedom from harassment and discrimination on the basis of race, ancestry, place of origin, colour, ethnic origin, citizenship, creed, sex, sexual orientation, age, marital status, family status, disability, or the receipt of public assistance. This legislation was originally passed in 1961 and has been changed several times by a simple majority vote in the Ontario legislature.

legislation: The act or process of making laws; also the laws made.

Responsibilities of Citizenship

Although the *Canadian Charter of Rights and Freedoms* does not outline any specific responsibilities for Canadians, the existence of rights always implies responsibilities:

- The right to protection by the law means you have the responsibility to obey the law.

- The right to vote in an election means you have the responsibility to stay informed about what governments are doing, about the views of political parties, and about the issues that are important in your community.

Informed citizens can make wise choices when voting in elections and participating in the democratic process. They help democracy work effectively.

Finally, some Canadians must take more direct responsibility for making democracy work: some Canadians must become candidates in elections, and be prepared to serve in Parliament or in their provincial legislatures if they are elected. Although not everyone needs to run for office, some people must, so that we have people to vote for and to lead our government.

▲ A candidate campaigns during the Ontario provincial election.

Voting

"I take my responsibilities as a citizen very seriously. When I cast my vote in an election, I have to know all about the different parties and what they say they will do. I usually study the newspapers and watch the television broadcasts to see what the party leaders have to say. Voting is really important to me because it's my chance to say what I think about how the country is being run."

"Who cares about voting? All the parties are the same. I can't be bothered reading about politics in the newspapers; I only read the sports pages. If the government ever did anything for me, I might vote; but they don't, so I never vote."

Questions

1. Which opinion do you favour? Why?
2. Assume the second opinion is correct. Why should citizens still vote?
3. Why is it your duty to vote as an informed citizen?

▲ A Canadian citizen casts his vote in a ballot box during a federal election. Many voting polls take place in school auditoriums.

Civics Now DVD

"A Father's Faith" from *Civics Now DVD*.

Making A Difference

John Diefenbaker

John Diefenbaker was prime minister of Canada from 1957 to 1963. He was a controversial politician who had a strong interest in protecting human rights. His greatest achievement was the passing of the *Canadian Bill of Rights* in 1960. This legislation marked the first time that the rights of Canadians were written out and passed into law at the federal level.

Questions

1. In your school, do you know what your rights and responsibilities are? Are they in writing?
2. Discuss with your class why it is important to have your rights and responsibilities written down.

▲ John Diefenbaker was a firm defender of human rights.

Web Links

John Diefenbaker

To learn more about John Diefenbaker, go to www.nelson.com/civicsnow.

↔ Check Your Understanding

1. What are the three ways that a person can become a Canadian citizen?
2. List three important rights that the *Charter* guarantees.
3. What are the advantages of stating basic rights and freedoms in the *Charter?* Which three rights do you think are the most important? Give reasons why.
4. Which of the following are "rights" under the *Canadian Charter of Rights and Freedoms?* In which cases would these rights affect the rights of others?

    a) the right to shout rude comments during a movie in a theatre

    b) the right to be protected from being beaten up

    c) the right to be free from sexual harassment

    d) the right to live in any province of Canada

Safety Versus Freedom

After the terrorist attacks on the United States on September 11, 2001, the Canadian government directed several billion dollars to protect Canada against terror attacks. Later, terror attacks in England, Spain, and other countries have resulted in more changes to our Canadian way of life. Security at airports is tighter, new immigrants are being more carefully screened, and passports will be required to travel between Canada and the United States for the first time in history.

In December 2001, the federal government passed an *Anti-terrorism Act.* The government stated that it was trying to reach a balance between Canadian values of fairness, respect for human rights and individual privacy, and the need for public safety. New laws gave police unlimited powers to arrest and detain travellers suspected of terrorist activities. They also forced people to give testimony in front of a judge without a formal trial.

Questions

1. Do you think giving up personal freedom for safety is a good tradeoff? Explain your answer.

2. Do you think that any particular groups in Canada are more likely to be affected by these laws? Explain your reasons. What would your reaction be to these measures if you were part of that group?

▲ Security officers are on alert at Pearson International Airport. After the terrorist attacks in the United States on September 11, 2001, it is common to see police officers at airports.

2.2 | Elections

Focus Question

- *How has democracy changed in Canada since 1867?*

franchise: The right of citizens of a country, such as Canada, to vote in their country's elections. The federal franchise is related to voting in federal elections.

Democracy in Canada has been changing since before the time of Confederation. What one generation of Canadians views as democratic, a new generation may see as repressive. For example, who has the right to vote? Today, we believe in the universal **franchise**; in other words, all citizens over the age of 18 have the right to vote. But this was not always the case. Throughout history, groups of people were refused the vote for a variety of reasons.

Timeline: The History of the Federal Franchise

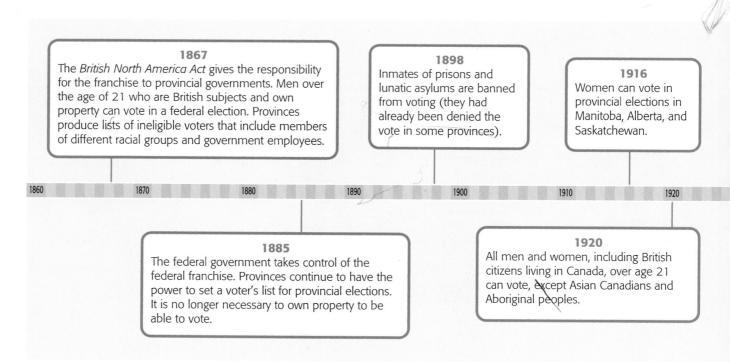

1867
The *British North America Act* gives the responsibility for the franchise to provincial governments. Men over the age of 21 who are British subjects and own property can vote in a federal election. Provinces produce lists of ineligible voters that include members of different racial groups and government employees.

1898
Inmates of prisons and lunatic asylums are banned from voting (they had already been denied the vote in some provinces).

1916
Women can vote in provincial elections in Manitoba, Alberta, and Saskatchewan.

1885
The federal government takes control of the federal franchise. Provinces continue to have the power to set a voter's list for provincial elections. It is no longer necessary to own property to be able to vote.

1920
All men and women, including British citizens living in Canada, over age 21 can vote, except Asian Canadians and Aboriginal peoples.

1860 1870 1880 1890 1900 1910 1920

During the years after Confederation, certain citizens were denied the right to vote because of race, sex, poverty, religion, age, employment, disability, and imprisonment. In Canadian law, some members of society were deemed less worthy than others.

For 10 of the first 13 federal elections, the right to vote was determined by the provincial governments. This meant that the rules deciding who could vote in a federal election were different depending on which province a person lived in. The timeline below illustrates some of the important changes in the right to vote in a federal election.

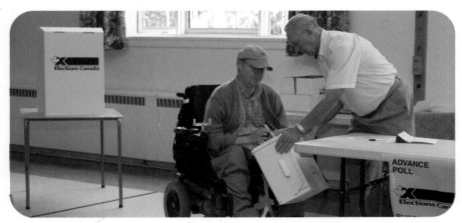

▲ A physically challenged citizen votes in a federal election. Polling stations were made accessible to disabled persons in 1992.

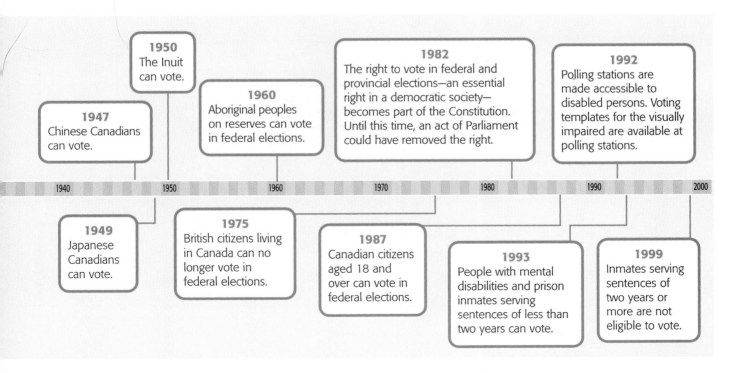

1947
Chinese Canadians can vote.

1950
The Inuit can vote.

1960
Aboriginal peoples on reserves can vote in federal elections.

1982
The right to vote in federal and provincial elections—an essential right in a democratic society—becomes part of the Constitution. Until this time, an act of Parliament could have removed the right.

1992
Polling stations are made accessible to disabled persons. Voting templates for the visually impaired are available at polling stations.

1940 — 1950 — 1960 — 1970 — 1980 — 1990 — 2000

1949
Japanese Canadians can vote.

1975
British citizens living in Canada can no longer vote in federal elections.

1987
Canadian citizens aged 18 and over can vote in federal elections.

1993
People with mental disabilities and prison inmates serving sentences of less than two years can vote.

1999
Inmates serving sentences of two years or more are not eligible to vote.

Difference

Nellie McClung

Nellie McClung was a tireless worker in the fight to get the vote for women. Many historians feel she was the leading Canadian feminist in the twentieth century. Well known as an engaging public speaker, she once gave a speech ridiculing the idea of votes for men, in order to poke fun at those who didn't support votes for women. Because of her work and that of many other women, Manitoba became the first province to give women the right to vote, in 1916, quickly followed by Alberta and Saskatchewan. In 1921, McClung was elected to the Manitoba legislature.

Questions

1. If you were to interview Nellie McClung, what three questions would you ask?
2. Do you think women should be given special status (e.g., the federal government agency Status of Women Canada)? Why or why not? Be prepared to defend your opinions.

▲ Nellie McClung was largely responsible for winning women the right to vote.

Getting Elected

Focus Question

- *How are candidates elected in Canada?*

Citizens often have a choice of several candidates when they vote. Usually, each candidate represents a political party. In Canada, both federally and provincially, candidates run for election in a **riding** (also called an **electoral district**). There are 308 federal ridings in Canada, and 103 provincial ridings in Ontario. The government determines all riding boundaries. Citizens living in a riding can vote for one representative to the federal Parliament and one to the provincial legislature. To be a candidate in a federal election, you must be

- a Canadian citizen
- 18 years of age or older

To run in a provincial election in Ontario, you have to be

- a Canadian citizen
- 18 years of age or older
- a resident of Ontario for at least six months before the election is called

riding: A defined area where voters elect a member of a legislature. An electoral district or constituency.

electoral district: A defined area where voters elect a member of a legislature. A riding.

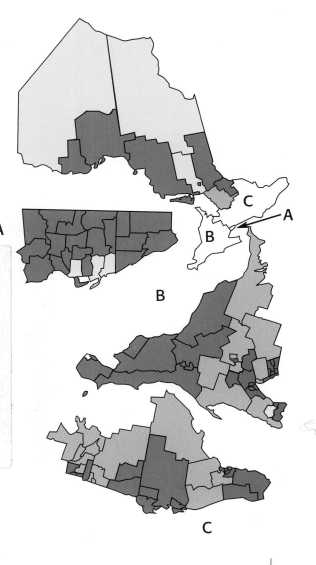

Ontario Provincial Electoral Districts

- New Democratic Party
- Liberal
- Progressive Conservative

▶ This is a map of the 103 electoral districts for the 2003 provincial election in Ontario. For the next provincial election in October 2007, Ontario will be divided into 107 electoral districts.

▲ This student is giving an election speech at her school. For many young people, student council elections are an introduction to the election process.

The Election Process

When we vote, we are choosing people to represent us in Parliament (federal) or in the provincial assemblies. They have a responsibility to speak for us. If the person we vote for wins, and if that person belongs to the party that wins the most seats, then that party will form the government. The leader of that party will then become the prime minister (in the federal government) or the premier (in a provincial government). In Canada, we do not vote directly for the person who becomes prime minister or premier.

The Call

The governor general (federal) or lieutenant governor (provincial) calls an election on the advice of the prime minister (federal) or premier (provincial). Federal governments can serve for up to five years. Previously, in Ontario, an election could be called any time, up to five years after the last election. Recently, the Ontario legislature set a fixed term of four years between general elections.

The Candidates

People who run in elections are called candidates. Many schools have a student council to voice the concerns of students and run school events. The council is made up of students chosen by their peers. To serve on the council, these students need to become candidates and run for election. A similar process takes place in elections for both the federal and provincial governments in Canada.

The Nominations

Candidates (usually representing political parties) submit **nominations** and run for election.

nomination: The process by which a person is selected to run for elected office.

The Voters' List

In Canada, and in each province, an official, known as the chief electoral officer, prepares the voters' list. It has the names of citizens who are eligible to vote. The chief electoral officer's job is also to publicize how voters can get their names on the voters' list.

The Campaign

Political parties campaign in the weeks before the election to promote their platforms (the things they say they will do if elected) to the voters. They use radio, newspaper, and television advertisements, leaflets, candidates' meetings, debates, appearances on television and radio shows, lawn signs, party Web sites, and visits to voters' homes. Federal and provincial laws govern the conduct of campaigns. These laws regulate the length of campaigns, access to television time, money spent by candidates and political parties, and other related matters.

The Voters

Citizens are told when and where they can vote and what to do if they think they may not be on the voters' list. These lists are posted in public areas such as government buildings and libraries.

The Decision

On the day of the election, voters go to polling stations, located in schools, community centres, and other public buildings. You may have seen polling stations in your school gym during the last election. Each polling station has a deputy returning officer who administers the voting, and a polling clerk who records the names of voters.

Voters cast a vote for the candidate of their choice by placing a mark beside the name on the ballot. The ballot, with the names of candidates, is refolded so that the choice is secret. The ballot is placed in a ballot box. How a voter voted remains secret unless the voter wants to tell others how he or she voted.

The Count

When the polls close, people, called counters, open the ballot boxes and count the votes. Members of the different political parties, called scrutineers, are present to make sure the count is fair.

The Winner

Candidates with the most votes in their ridings are declared the winners. These candidates become the representatives for the ridings in Parliament or in the provincial assemblies.

Web Links

Research Your Riding
To find your riding, go to **www.nelson.com/civicsnow** and follow the instructions. Who were the candidates in the last election? Who won?

Literacy Strategy

After you have finished reading these two pages, pause and think about them. Summarize the content in your own words, or sketch the information to make sure you understand the content.

↔ Check Your Understanding

1. Which of the changes to the federal franchise listed in the timeline do you think is the most important? Justify your choice.

2. Name five steps in the election process. In your own words, describe their importance.

3. Interview a local elected representative (provincial or federal) and ask him or her about his or her experiences in running in a recent election. Write a report and present it to your class.

2.3 | Parliament and Government

The Three Levels of Government

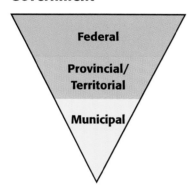

- Federal
- Provincial/ Territorial
- Municipal

Focus Question

- How are federal and provincial governments organized in Canada?

Canada is a parliamentary democracy in which people elect individuals to represent them in Parliament. Power—and the responsibility for making laws, regulations, policies, and decisions—is divided between the federal government and those of the provinces. This is called a federal system. The Constitution outlines the responsibilities of the federal and provincial governments. Some of these responsibilities overlap.

Making A Difference

Sir John A. Macdonald

Sir John A. Macdonald was one of the Fathers of Confederation and Canada's first prime minister. He believed in a strong central government and would have preferred to give the provinces little or no power. Other powerful leaders argued that strong provinces were necessary to preserve local culture and tradition. The eventual compromise on a federal structure was necessary to achieve Confederation.

▲ Sir John A. Macdonald wanted a strong federal government.

Question

Do you agree or disagree with Sir John A. Macdonald that a strong central government is important? Explain your reasoning.

We often think of municipalities as a third level of government. City, town, and community governments have many of the features of federal and provincial governments, but the provincial governments can create, abolish, or change the powers and responsibilities of municipalities.

Ecohabits

Government and Students Work Together to Protect Local Lakes

Different municipal governments vary in their levels of environmental awareness and action. Sometimes, when confronted with an environmental issue, municipal governments come up with creative strategies for involving students in the solution. The Township of Muskoka Lakes has worked closely with the residents to develop an action plan for protecting the local lakes from pollution, including

- passing municipal laws, or bylaws, on sewage disposal systems
- conducting information campaigns

- hiring students from local high schools to perform a sanitary survey on the most critical areas—for example, soap, shampoo, and other household cleaning products
- following up the survey with corrections through its bylaw enforcement officers
- promoting a boycott on detergents by hiring students to visit each cottage and trade a box of phosphate-free soap for the cottager's detergent
- passing bylaws to limit development of at-risk environmental locations on the waterfront

Question

Discuss with your class how you can make a difference to the environment in your community. Give specific examples.

◀ Clean water, like this lake in Muskoka, is important to our environment and our community. Young people can help protect the local environment from pollution.

Government Organization

Canada is a constitutional monarchy based on the British model, which is why the queen is the head of the Canadian government. Since the queen is rarely in Canada, the governor general represents her at the federal level and a lieutenant governor represents her in each province.

Within Canada, three branches of government exist at both the federal and the provincial levels: the executive, the legislative, and the judiciary.

The Three Branches of Government in Canada

Branches	Federal	Provincial
Executive	Queen (Governor General)	Lieutenant Governor (Queen)
	Prime Minister	Premier
	Federal Cabinet	Cabinet
	Civil Service	Civil Service
Legislative	Parliament	Provincial Legislature
	Governor General (Queen)	Lieutenant Governor (Queen)
	House of Commons	Elected house
	Senate	
Judiciary	Federal Judiciary	Provincial Judiciary

The Federal Parliament

In the parliamentary system of government, voters give the power to make new laws and regulations to elected Members of Parliament. The federal Parliament consists of the queen (represented by the governor general), an elected House of Commons, and an appointed Senate. At both the federal and provincial levels, the elected legislatures are organized in the same way.

▲ This is the Supreme Court of Canada building in Ottawa.

The Queen

In our constitutional monarchy, the queen is the head of state. She is represented by the governor general at the federal level, and a lieutenant governor in each province. Although her role is now mainly ceremonial, she is still an important part of our government. In order for bills to become law, they must receive royal assent (signing) by the queen or her representative.

The Governor General

The governor general and the lieutenant governors represent the queen as head of state. No bill, federal or provincial, becomes law without being signed by the governor general at the federal level or the lieutenant governor at the provincial level. This is known as royal assent. The queen's representatives are ceremonial positions with little actual power or authority.

▲ Queen Elizabeth II is Canada's head of state.

Parts of Our Government
For a good overview of the many parts of our government system, go to **www.nelson.com/civicsnow.**

▲ Governor General Michaëlle Jean was appointed in September 2005. She represents the queen in Canada as head of state.

The Senate

The Senate is part of our Parliament. It is not elected. The governor general, "on the recommendation of the prime minister," appoints its members. This means that the prime minister does the actual appointing, and the governor general approves each appointment. The Senate reviews and suggests changes to legislation passed by the House of Commons. In theory, it has the power to refuse to pass legislation from the House of Commons, but it does this very rarely.

Let's Discuss

The role of the Senate has long been the subject of controversy. Some people want the Senate abolished, while others would like to see senators elected. Research the role of the Senate and list three reasons why you think it should be abolished and three reasons why you think it should be kept.

Civics Now DVD

"Senators in Waiting" from *Civics Now DVD*.

House of Commons

Like the Senate, the House of Commons is part of Parliament. However, it is elected. It is the most powerful branch of Parliament. Here are the key people in the federal House of Commons:

Members of Parliament (MPs)

Members of Parliament, as a group, are referred to as the House of Commons. MPs meet in the House of Commons to debate and vote on proposed legislation. MPs are elected to represent voters in a particular riding. They are usually members of a political party and vote and act the way their party leader tells them to. MPs who belong to or support the party that forms the government sit on the government side of the House of Commons. Other MPs are members of the opposition parties, and they sit on the opposite side.

Speaker of the House

The speaker of the house is an MP elected by MPs. He or she is responsible for keeping order in debates and makes many decisions on the day-to-day running of the House of Commons.

Prime Minister

The prime minister is usually the leader of the political party that has the most seats in the House of Commons. He or she is the most powerful person in Parliament.

Cabinet Ministers

The prime minister selects ministers to be responsible for different areas. All of these ministers together are known as the cabinet. They are usually chosen from the MPs of the prime minister's own party, but on some occasions, Senators have served in the cabinet. The prime minister and the cabinet direct government policy.

Leader of the Official Opposition

The leader of the official opposition is usually the leader of the second-largest party in Parliament. He or she is responsible for presenting clear alternatives to government policy.

Shadow Cabinet

Members of the shadow cabinet criticize government policy. They take on the same areas of responsibility as ministers of the actual cabinet.

Civics Now DVD

"Parliamentary Tour" from *Civics Now DVD*.

Parliament

To get an active view of your federal Parliament and discover who does what, go to **www.nelson.com/civicsnow**.

The House of Commons

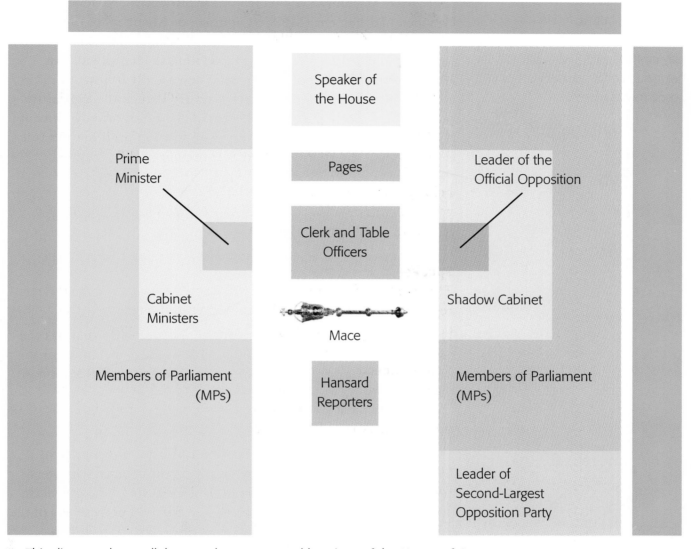

Speaker of the House

Pages

Clerk and Table Officers

Prime Minister

Leader of the Official Opposition

Cabinet Ministers

Mace

Shadow Cabinet

Members of Parliament (MPs)

Hansard Reporters

Members of Parliament (MPs)

Leader of Second-Largest Opposition Party

▲ This diagram shows all the members, parts, and locations of the House of Commons.

A Provincial Legislature

The provincial governments consist of the lieutenant governor (representing the queen) and an elected legislature. Many of the roles in the provincial legislature mirror those at the federal level. Here are the key people in a provincial legislature (sometimes referred to as a provincial Parliament):

Members of the Provincial Legislatures

Members of the provincial legislatures include Members of the Legislative Assembly (MLAs) (for most provinces), Members of the Provincial Parliament (MPPs) (Ontario), or Members of the National Assembly (MNAs) (Quebec). These people are elected to represent and serve the voters in their ridings. They are almost always members of a political party. They usually follow the instructions of their party leader when they vote in the legislature. If their party forms the government, they will support government policy. If their party forms one of the opposition parties, their role is to present clear alternatives to government policy.

Speaker of the House

The speaker of the house is a member of the legislature who is elected by his or her peers by secret ballot. She or he is responsible for keeping order in debates, and makes many decisions on the day-to-day running of the legislature.

Premier

The premier is usually the leader of the political party that has the most seats in the legislature. Comparable to the prime minister in the federal Parliament, the premier is the most powerful person in the legislature.

Cabinet Ministers

The premier selects ministers to be responsible for different areas. All of these ministers together are known as the cabinet. Ministers are usually chosen from members of the legislature of the premier's own party. They may, however, be chosen from other members of the legislature. The premier and the cabinet direct government policy.

Leader of the Official Opposition

The leader of the official opposition is usually the leader of the second-largest party in the legislature. This person is responsible for criticizing and putting forward alternatives to government policy.

Shadow Cabinet

The leader of the official opposition selects the shadow cabinet. Its job is to "shadow" the cabinet by criticizing government policy. Members of the shadow cabinet take on the same areas of responsibility as members of the cabinet.

Web Links

The Ontario Legislative Assembly

To view some photos and artifacts regarding the Ontario legislature, go to www.nelson.com/civicsnow.

A Provincial Legislature

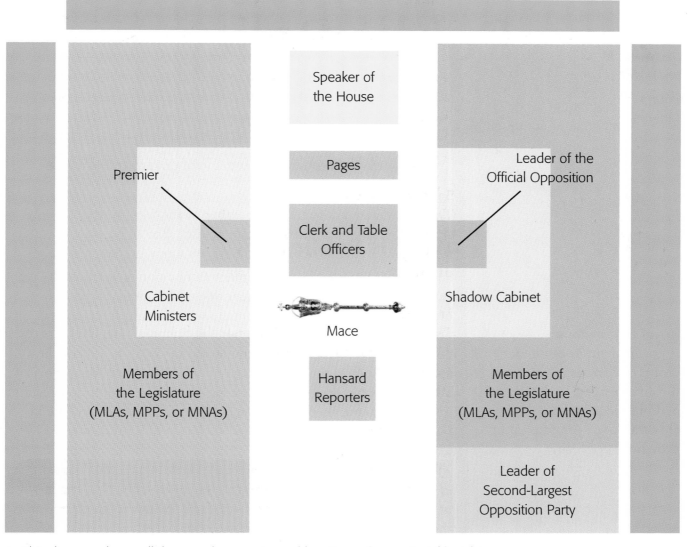

Speaker of
the House

Pages

Clerk and Table
Officers

Premier

Cabinet
Ministers

Mace

Leader of the
Official Opposition

Shadow Cabinet

Members of
the Legislature
(MLAs, MPPs, or MNAs)

Hansard
Reporters

Members of
the Legislature
(MLAs, MPPs, or MNAs)

Leader of
Second-Largest
Opposition Party

▲ This diagram shows all the members, parts, and locations of a provincial legislature.

↔ Check Your Understanding

1. List three responsibilities of the federal government and a provincial government.
2. Describe the role of the Senate, the governor general, and the speaker of the house.

2.4 | Public Policy

Focus Question

- *How do the federal and provincial governments make public policy?*

What Is Public Policy?

Royal Commission:
A government-appointed group of citizens responsible for investigating in detail and making recommendations about an issue of national or provincial concern.

Every government sets public policy. Public policy is a broad statement of what the government does. Each political party presents a platform of its ideas at election time, and these ideas often form the basis for public policy if the party forms a government. Of course, governments do not have to follow the agenda laid out in their election platform. Sometimes the report of a **Royal Commission** or another type of public consultation results in changes to public policy. New public policy may also come in response to a variety of problems, such as a natural disaster.

▲ Public consultation is important in changing public policy. Here, panellists discuss the SARS epidemic of 2003 at a Health Canada conference in Toronto.

The Civil Service

Both federal and provincial civil services do many things for the government and citizens of Canada. Governments use their civil servants to carry out the policies they pass in Parliament.

Civil servants occupy many roles, ranging from teachers, doctors, and nurses, to ministry employees and experts in specific fields. Our system of government could not function without these workers.

Cabinet ministers need the expertise of civil servants so they can run their departments. Because civil servants often spend considerable time in their jobs, they are able to contribute experience that a cabinet minister, who may serve for a short time, may not have. It is the civil service that ensures that governments run efficiently.

▲ Parks Canada civil servants receive search-and-rescue training.

Ministries and Public Policy

The prime minister and cabinet are responsible for setting government policy. Within the cabinet, ministers usually take responsibility for specific departments, such as finance, transportation, and agriculture. Ministers often compete for funds for their own departments, in order to pay for new government programs. Ministers who have great political influence or are in the most powerful departments have the most effect on public policy.

Governments want to be reelected, so they often pass popular new laws, such as tax cuts or public spending in key areas, just before the next election. When an election loomed in Ottawa in late 2005, the Minister of Finance, Ralph Goodale, delivered what was called a mini-budget. In it, the Liberal government offered $30 billion in tax cuts to Canadian citizens. They also promised to spend money on education, immigration, and other areas they hoped voters would appreciate. This sort of popular spending is common just before elections.

A government is more likely to introduce unpopular legislation at the beginning or in the middle of its term. The party in power always hopes voters have short memories and forget past mistakes and unpopular legislation, and remember only the most recent, popular accomplishments.

Let's Discuss

In your own experience, have you ever promised to do something in order to get something in return? Share your experiences with the class.

Let's Discuss

Name something you did last weekend that was made possible by the government. Which level of government (federal, provincial, or municipal) was responsible for that activity? Compare and discuss with a classmate.

Dividing the Duties of Government

The following chart shows Canada's three levels of government, and some of the duties of each. In different places, different ministries or agencies are responsible for some of these duties. As well, some duties, such as taking care of natural resources, are shared.

Canada's Three Levels of Government and Some of Their Duties

Federal	*Provincial/Territorial*	*Municipal*
• trade • post office • census • copyright • national defence • employment insurance • money and banking • criminal law • citizenship • foreign affairs	• natural resources and environment • highways • health, hospitals • property and civil rights • education • labour • social services • municipal government	• water • sewage • waste collection • public transit • land use planning • libraries • ambulances • animal control • development of local economy

Functions of Government

Focus Question

- *What are the powers and functions of the federal, provincial, and municipal governments?*

Canada's Constitution outlines specific responsibilities for the federal and provincial governments.

Federal Responsibilities

Federal responsibilities affect the entire country. These include

- financial, monetary, and economic policy
- taxation
- borrowing money for government spending
- national defence
- foreign affairs
- trade
- criminal laws and penitentiaries
- shipping and navigation
- sea coast and inland fisheries
- international and interprovincial ferries
- employment insurance
- citizenship
- postal service
- census
- copyright
- areas not specifically assigned to the provinces by the Constitution

Provincial Responsibilities

A provincial government has important responsibilities for services and laws that affect Canadians in that province. These include

- elementary, secondary, and postsecondary education
- direct taxation for provincial uses
- provincial prisons
- health care
- management of natural resources
- supervision of municipalities
- construction and maintenance of highways
- workers' compensation programs
- labour
- social services

Let's Discuss

Each level of government has its own responsibilities. Many clubs or teams also have levels of responsibilities, or duties. Make a list of duties in one of your clubs or teams. Who is in charge of each duty? Compare your list with a classmate's.

▲ Prime Minister Jean Chrétien refused to take part in the invasion of Iraq in 2003. This decision was a defining moment in Canadian foreign policy.

Jean Chrétien

Foreign affairs is a federal responsibility. When the United States led the invasion of Iraq in 2003, Prime Minister Jean Chrétien refused to send Canadian troops without the approval of the United Nations. This was not the first time that the Canadian federal government disagreed with American foreign policy. However, it was a very important and controversial decision. Many prominent Americans denounced Prime Minister Chrétien and Canada because of it.

Questions

1. Research the causes of the Iraqi war. Do you agree with Prime Minister Jean Chrétien's decision not to be part of this invasion? Why or why not? Be prepared to defend your response.

2. Research other times that Canada disagreed with American foreign policy. Discuss your findings with the class.

Shared Responsibilities

Certain responsibilities are shared between federal and provincial governments. These include

- the judicial system
- agriculture and farming
- old-age security
- immigration
- environmental protection

When governments disagree about which one is in charge of an area, they usually try to settle these disputes through negotiation. If they do not succeed, the courts may be asked to interpret the Constitution to decide which level of government has jurisdiction.

Both federal and provincial governments collect taxes to pay for the programs and services they provide. The federal government also shares some of its tax revenues with poorer provinces. These payments are known as equalization payments because they try to equalize the wealth of all provinces. The federal government also pays part of the cost of health care and education, even though these are provincial responsibilities.

Municipal Responsibilities

In Canada, provincial legislation states how the governments of over 5000 cities, towns, villages, counties, districts, and metropolitan regions are set. It defines the powers of municipal governments and states how mayors and their officials are elected.

Municipal governments provide their citizens with vital and daily services including

- water supply, sewage treatment, and garbage disposal
- road and sidewalk maintenance and construction
- street lights, parks, playgrounds, and libraries
- policies, such as building codes and bylaws
- police and fire departments

Although many consider this third level of government perhaps less important than the other two, municipal services affect the lives of Canadian citizens in a very important way.

▲ Municipal governments provide many important services, such as this basketball court in a public park.

Municipal Government in Action

What Your Municipal Government Does for You	Examples
provides services	policing, fire protection, public transit, and libraries
passes bylaws	to control traffic, parking, garbage, noise, and pet ownership
develops the community	attracts tourism and business to the community through special events, such as fairs, exhibits, and sporting events
makes decisions	builds bridges, roads, and community centres; starts recycling programs

Federal Laws and Regulations

Focus Question

- *How do the federal and provincial governments make laws and regulations?*

▲ Governor General Adrienne Clarkson reads the Speech from the Throne in October 2004.

Speech from the Throne: A statement of the legislative program or bills that a provincial or federal government intends to pass in the coming session of Parliament. The speech is delivered by the lieutenant governor or governor general to the assembled legislature.

bill: A document that outlines a new law to be set before Parliament for consideration.

The federal Parliament meets at least once a year to debate policy and make laws. The federal government has a responsibility to propose legislation and make public policy that benefits all Canadians.

Before any laws are made, the prime minister and the cabinet plan the government's legislative agenda for the upcoming session of Parliament. This agenda outlines the government's plan for new laws and what actions it intends to take.

The governor general reads this legislative agenda to Parliament in the **Speech from the Throne**. In the Speech from the Throne, the government communicates its plans to Parliament and the public. The Speech from the Throne is followed by a parliamentary debate that lasts for a number of days and gives the opposition parties the opportunity to critique the government's agenda.

Moving a Bill Through Parliament

When the prime minister and cabinet, along with the civil service, see a need for change in certain laws or regulations, they write these ideas down using legal terminology and draft them in the form of a **bill**. The bill is then presented to Parliament to be voted into law or rejected. When the party in power has a majority of the seats in the House of Commons, it will easily pass the bill into law.

The process is slightly more complicated when there is a minority government. When the government does not have a clear majority, it must negotiate to gain the support of one or more of the opposition parties to get enough votes to pass the bill.

Occasionally, if rarely, governments sometimes allow bills, such as the recent same-sex marriage legislation, to be decided by what is known as an "open vote." This means members from all parties can vote the way they want rather than the way the party tells them to vote.

Moving a Bill Through Parliament

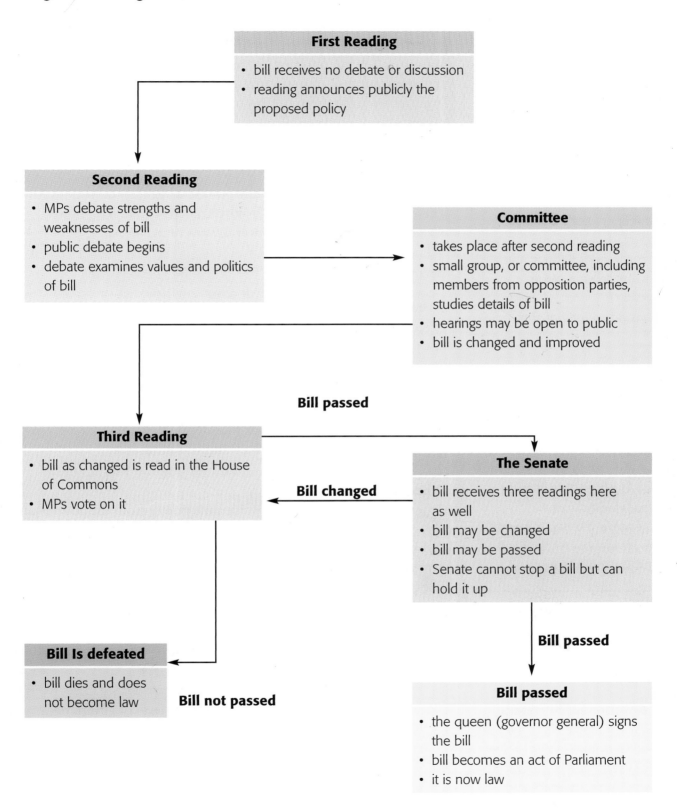

First Reading
- bill receives no debate or discussion
- reading announces publicly the proposed policy

Second Reading
- MPs debate strengths and weaknesses of bill
- public debate begins
- debate examines values and politics of bill

Committee
- takes place after second reading
- small group, or committee, including members from opposition parties, studies details of bill
- hearings may be open to public
- bill is changed and improved

Bill passed

Third Reading
- bill as changed is read in the House of Commons
- MPs vote on it

Bill changed

The Senate
- bill receives three readings here as well
- bill may be changed
- bill may be passed
- Senate cannot stop a bill but can hold it up

Bill passed

Bill Is defeated
- bill dies and does not become law

Bill not passed

Bill passed
- the queen (governor general) signs the bill
- bill becomes an act of Parliament
- it is now law

Provincial Laws and Regulations

Provincial governments operate much the same way as the federal government. One difference, though, is that provincial legislatures do not have a Senate, or other "upper" chamber. The federal Senate has the important task of suggesting changes to bills. At the provincial level, following the second reading of a bill, a **committee** reviews and suggests changes to the bill.

Agencies

Governments often give agencies power to regulate certain activities. These agencies are often run by government appointees, not by elected members. There are several types of agencies.

Occupational Groups

Occupational groups, such as doctors, engineers, lawyers, and teachers, have the power to decide who will be allowed to enter their profession. They can also decide on disciplinary action that could result in the expulsion of a member.

Marketing Boards

There are many marketing boards. For example, farmers have the power to run marketing boards that decide how much of a given product each farmer can produce and its selling price.

Other Agencies

Other agencies that receive considerable power from the government are the National Parole Board and the Human Rights Tribunal. The Parole Board has the power to decide when a prisoner can be given parole, and the conditions of his or her release. The Human Rights Tribunal decides whether a person's rights as defined by the *Canadian Charter of Rights and Freedoms* have been violated, and can make recommendations for action to be taken to correct an injustice.

↔ Check Your Understanding

1. List the major responsibilities of each level of government.
2. How does a bill become law in the federal Parliament?
3. Is the process of moving a bill through so many steps really effective? Why or why not?

2.5 | Political Parties

Parties in Canadian Democracy

Political parties play a major role in Canadian democracy. In a modern parliamentary democracy like ours, voters must be allowed to choose a candidate. Choice is an essential ingredient to a democracy. If only one candidate runs in an election, the citizens have no choice. However, if every candidate has his or her own opinion on every issue, there would be mass confusion. Political parties help candidates group themselves according to shared beliefs, and help voters know what those beliefs are.

Each political party develops a statement of ideas, policies, and beliefs called a platform, which tells what the party plans to do if it forms the next government. For example, most parties would say reducing crime is a priority; however, each party may have different ideas about how this can be achieved. These ideas are outlined in the party's platform.

Political parties have several other important functions:

- They give citizens a way to work together and to influence government and public policy.
- They simplify the way the government, prime minister, and cabinet are selected.
- They recruit people who agree with their ideas to run as candidates in elections.
- They limit the number of things a government could do while in office by stating a clear set of policies to present to the voters.

political parties: Organized groups with similar ideas about government and politics who run candidates for office and who seek to form a government.

Civics Now DVD

"Green Backstory" from *Civics Now DVD*.

Political Parties
To visit the Web sites of the main political parties, go to **www.nelson.com/civicsnow**. Create a visual organizer to compare and contrast three of the party platforms.

2004 Federal Election Results

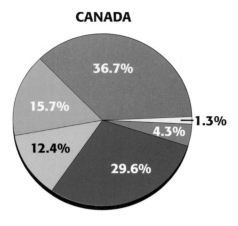

CANADA

36.7%
15.7%
1.3%
4.3%
12.4%
29.6%

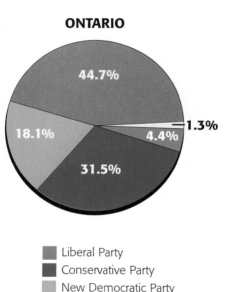

ONTARIO

44.7%
18.1%
1.3%
4.4%
31.5%

- Liberal Party
- Conservative Party
- New Democratic Party
- Bloc Québécois
- Green Party
- Others

Let's Discuss

Have you read, seen, or heard anything in the media lately about the changes in Canadian politics? Research and list three recent important changes. Discuss your findings in class.

Canada has many political parties. Some exist at the federal level, some at the provincial level, and some at both levels of government. Some federal parties are regional. For example, the Bloc Québécois is a federal party that tries to gain seats only in Quebec. Other federal parties, such as the Liberal Party, the Conservative Party of Canada, and the New Democratic Party, try to win seats across the country.

The Evolving Party System

The party system is evolving. For more than half a century after Confederation, Canada had only two federal parties—the Liberals and the Conservatives. They were joined in the 1930s by the Co-operative Commonwealth Federation (CCF), an association of farm and labour groups. The CCF and the Canadian Labour Congress joined together to form the New Democratic Party in 1961. In October 2003, the Canadian Alliance and the Progressive Conservative Parties joined together to form the new Conservative Party of Canada, under the leadership of Stephen Harper.

Regional and Special Interest Parties

Regional and special interest parties have played an important role in the evolution of the Canadian political system. They provide a reminder of the need to address regional issues and those of special interest groups. Over the years, Canadian politics have seen numerous regional parties, including the Social Credit Party, Progressive Party, Reform Party of Canada, and Canadian Reform Conservative Alliance.

Another regional party that has had some success is the Bloc Québécois. Formed in 1991 to represent Quebec's interests in Ottawa, within two years it was the official opposition. Now the third-largest party, after the Liberals and the Conservatives, the Bloc makes no attempt to become a national party. Its aim is to promote the separation of Quebec from the rest of Canada. The Parti Québécois is strictly a provincial party and does not run in federal elections. It has formed the government in Quebec in the past.

Independents

A small number of members in the House of Commons are not part of any political party. These members are known as independents. In 2005, the minority Liberal government depended on the votes of the independents to avoid being defeated.

Majority Governments

The ultimate goal of the major political parties is to have enough candidates elected to form a majority government. A majority government occurs when a political party wins more than half the ridings in an election.

The party with the greatest number of seats forms the government. When an election is called, political parties try to get their candidates elected in as many ridings as possible.

In the 2003 provincial election in Ontario, the Liberal Party led by Dalton McGuinty won 72 seats. The Progressive Conservative Party won 24 seats, and the New Democratic Party won 7 seats. This gave the Liberals a majority of 41 seats (72 − 24 + 7), and allowed them to form a majority government. As a result of this majority, the lieutenant governor of Ontario asked Dalton McGuinty to form the next government.

The fact that a party forms a majority government does not always mean that that party has won a majority of the **popular vote**. The party with the most votes in any riding wins the seat. Because the popular vote is divided among three or more parties, a party may win a majority of seats with less than half the popular vote. For example, in the 1984 federal election, the Progressive Conservatives won about half of the popular vote but gained about three-quarters of the seats in the House of Commons. Because voter turnout is very low in Canadian elections (only about 60 percent), a political party could possibly form a majority government with the support of only about a third of eligible voters.

▲ In October 2003, Dalton McGuinty was elected premier of Ontario and won a majority. Here, he celebrates his victory with his wife, Terri.

popular vote: The total number of votes cast by voters in an election.

Minority Governments

A minority government occurs when a political party elects more members to Parliament or the provincial legislature than any other party, but not more than all the other parties added together. The governor general or lieutenant governor will usually ask the leader of this party to form the next government.

The leader of the party with the most seats becomes the next prime minister or premier and selects a cabinet from members elected from his or her party. But, in a minority government, the party in power has to rely on the votes of members of other parties to pass its legislation.

Civics Now DVD

"Spin City"
from *Civics Now DVD*.

Minority and Coalition Governments

In 2004, Paul Martin's Liberals failed to win an overall majority in the general election. They won only 135 of 308 seats, but were able to continue as a minority government, thanks to the prime minister's ability to "wheel and deal." For a while, he was able to offer parties something they wanted if they would support his government. But in November 2005, the opposition parties united to defeat the Martin government. An election was called for January 2006.

A minority government may make a deal with another party to support it on a more permanent basis, rather than having to constantly make deals. This is known as a coalition government. For example, in the 1999 Saskatchewan election, the NDP government, led by Roy Romanow, lost its majority in the legislature. The Liberal Party, which gained just three seats, held the balance of power. Since the other two parties were evenly divided, the small Liberal Party had the power to break the tie. They entered into a coalition with the NDP, and members of these two parties formed Saskatchewan's government.

Questions

1. Discuss the pros and cons of minority and coalition governments.

2. Is there a downside for a party that supports a minority government or enters into a coalition with a larger party?

▲ Paul Martin, seated, failed to win a majority government in 2004. He was able to remain in power for 17 months by making deals with other parties.

Political Ideology in Canadian Politics

Some countries have political parties with extreme differences in **political ideology**—the beliefs that are part of their political systems. In Canada, the mainstream political parties (e.g., Liberal and Conservative) have traditionally been moderate.

Although these parties come from different ideological roots, they have often followed common policies. For example, free trade was traditionally part of a Liberal agenda, yet a Conservative government signed the North American Free Trade Agreement in 1988, and the Liberal Party opposed it. In the 1990s, the Liberal government of Prime Minister Jean Chrétien carried out a series of cuts to public spending, a policy more easily identified with a Conservative agenda.

The New Democratic Party has never been elected federally, but has been successful in several provinces. NDP governments have tended to stress public spending and government programs, such as welfare and medicare, that help the "average person."

Sometimes, governments are criticized when they follow policies that do not seem to reflect their parties' ideological values. The NDP government, led by Bob Rae in Ontario (1990–95), was faced with economic hardships. It introduced policies more conservative than those usually associated with the NDP and was defeated in the 1995 election.

political ideology: The system of ideas or beliefs about government that guides a person or political party.

▲ When Bob Rae was premier of Ontario, he made some drastic spending cuts.

↔ *Check Your Understanding*

1. List five major functions of political parties.
2. List the political parties that currently make up
   a) the federal government
   b) the federal opposition
   c) your provincial government
   d) your provincial opposition
3. Choose one of the parties above. Go to its official Web site and write three or four paragraphs that outline its key ideas and policies.

Literacy Strategy

After reading this section, you may wish to create a chart to help you sum up what you have learned about the people and events in Canadian politics.

The Judicial System

Duties of Courts

Canadian courts are the judicial branch of the government. One of their main tasks is to interpret the laws made and administered by the legislative and executive branches. They also settle disputes between individuals—on contract and property issues or family matters—as well as conflicts between individuals and the government, and between the different levels of government. Our courts have a duty to be **impartial**.

impartial: Fair and free of bias.

Judges

An important element of the judicial system is the independence of judges in the federal and provincial courts. To safeguard their independence, judges are protected from dismissal. In theory, it is possible to remove a judge from office, but this has never occurred in any Canadian superior court, although some judges have resigned during misconduct hearings. Judges continue to work until they resign or retire, as late as 75 years of age. This means they can make judgments without the fear of being removed if politicians do not like what they decide. This enables them to judge cases fairly and impartially.

Canadian judges are appointed. By contrast, some American states elect some judges. In Canada, some people argue that because our judges are appointed, they do not have to make decisions that are popular in order to get reelected. Others argue that because politicians appoint judges, they may be chosen for their political views rather than because of their merit or skill.

Web Links

Courts and Judges
To learn more about the Supreme Court of Canada and the judiciary in Canada, go to
www.nelson.com/civicsnow.

The Court System

The federal government is in charge of the Supreme Court of Canada and the Federal Court of Canada. The provinces or territories are in charge of all other courts. Each court has a different role or function. The following chart shows the Ontario court system.

The Ontario Court System

Supreme Court of Canada

- senior court in the land
- final appeal court for all civil and criminal cases
- hears appeals from the Federal Court and the provincial Superior Courts of Justice
- addresses constitutional issues referred by the federal government
- able to be selective about the cases it hears; therefore, it concentrates on issues of national importance

Federal Court

- deals with income tax, patents, customs cases, and immigration

Court of Ontario

Superior Court of Justice
- has jurisdiction over criminal prosecutions of indictable offences
- has jurisdiction over criminal prosecutions involving young persons

Divisional Court
- reviews decisions of administrative boards, tribunals, and public servants

Court of Appeal for Ontario
- hears requests to change or overturn decisions made by lower courts

Small Claims Court

- settles claims worth up to $10 000

Ontario Court of Justice

Criminal Law Division
- deals with people charged in 96 percent of criminal offences
- deals with minor offences in provincial law (these are usually presided over by Justices of the Peace)
- deals with youths charged under *Youth Criminal Justice Act*

Family Court
- deals with family matters (child custody, divorce)

Justice of the Peace
- deals with bail hearings
- has jurisdiction over prosecutions of provincial offences

Flaws in the System

The judicial system is not perfect. Sometimes, innocent citizens have been convicted of crimes by mistake. One of the best-known examples of this is the case of David Milgaard.

In 1969, 16-year-old Milgaard was arrested for the rape and murder of Gail Miller. Milgaard and some friends had stopped in Saskatoon en route to Alberta. On January 31, 1969, Miller's stabbed body was found in Saskatoon. The police posted a reward for information. Three months later, Milgaard's friends told the police that Milgaard had committed the crime. They said that Milgaard had blood on his clothing on the morning of the crime. Milgaard was arrested.

At the trial, the prosecution argued that Milgaard had become separated for 20 minutes from the others when their car was stuck in heavy snow. This happened about the same time of Miller's death. One of the three teenagers stated that she had witnessed Milgaard stabbing Miller. Milgaard was convicted of first-degree murder.

Milgaard spent the next 23 years in federal penitentiaries. His mother, Joyce, devoted herself to gathering evidence to prove his innocence. Helped by organizations and a sympathetic Winnipeg law firm, the family finally won Milgaard's freedom when the Supreme Court of Canada overturned the conviction. One of the key witnesses admitted to lying at the original trial. The others contradicted themselves when recalling the events of the day Miller was murdered.

In 1999, Larry Fisher, the real killer, was convicted from DNA evidence. David Milgaard was given a cash settlement of $10 million by the Saskatchewan government for the 23 years that he spent in Canada's penitentiaries.

▲ This is David Milgaard, in about 1993, after being released from prison, where he spent 23 years for a crime he did not commit.

Questions
1. How can cases such as Milgaard's be used as arguments against capital punishment, or the death sentence?
2. How would a modern Crime Scene Investigation Unit have helped to establish David Milgaard's innocence? Support your answer with specific evidence.

Protecting Our Rights

Focus Question

- *How does the judicial system protect the rights of individuals and society?*

Our judicial system protects the rights of individuals in several different ways:

- Everyone is presumed innocent until proven guilty. This long-held principle of Canadian law is now part of the *Canadian Charter of Rights and Freedoms.*

- Courts operate in public. Their proceedings are open for the public to see that they work fairly and follow the rules of law.

- An individual cannot be charged with breaking a law that was not in place when the offence occurred.

- No one can be forced to testify as a witness at his or her own trial.

- All accused people have a right to a lawyer, if they wish. If they cannot afford one, the government will pay for one.

The judicial system protects the rights of society by enforcing or reinterpreting written laws. Laws set out expected behaviour from individuals. Should these laws be broken, the judicial system is responsible for providing punishment and rehabilitation. By enforcing laws, the judicial system discourages unacceptable behaviour.

The courts must balance the protection of the rights of individuals against the rights of society—a difficult job. The *Canadian Charter of Rights and Freedoms* makes individual rights part of the Constitution. It also recognizes collective rights for linguistic minorities, Aboriginals, and other groups.

The following Civics Showcase shows how the courts have applied the *Canadian Charter of Rights and Freedoms* to balance the rights of individuals and the rights of society.

Civics Now DVD

"Sexual Offenders" from *Civics Now DVD.*

▲ The courts must balance the rights of individuals and the rights of society.

The Right to Vote

Prior to 1993, no citizens found guilty of criminal offences were allowed to vote in federal elections. Robert Rowbotham, imprisoned for 17 years, challenged this law. He believed that it violated his rights under the *Canadian Charter of Rights and Freedoms.* In March 1992, the Federal Court of Appeal agreed with Rowbotham.

After this, the *Canada Elections Act* was changed. It gave 21 000 prisoners who were serving sentences of less than two years the right to vote in federal elections.

On October 31, 2002, the Supreme Court decided that all federal prisoners should be allowed to vote. There are 13 000 federal prisoners who are serving two years or more. The Canadian government was not happy with the decision. "If you kill someone and you're in prison for life, you have the right to vote,"

▲ Canadian federal prisoners now have the right to vote. Here, a prisoner votes at a penitentiary.

a government spokesperson said. "But, if you leave the country for five years, to work or visit, you don't have the right to vote."

Question
Do you think prisoners should have the right to vote? Why or why not?

↔ Check Your Understanding

1. What are three main roles and responsibilities of the courts?

2. Describe how the judicial system protects the rights of individuals and society. Create a chart that lists three key points.

3. Should prisoners doing time in our penal systems have the same rights that all Canadians have before the law? Why or why not?

4. Research the legal system in Canada. Do we need to reform our legal system to prevent punishing innocent people? Support your answer with examples of some errors made in the past with our legal system.

Skills for Social Action

Role-plays

Role-plays are an exciting and engaging way to explore civics issues. You could develop the persona of a famous historical figure or a contemporary citizen. You might reenact an issue of civic conflict. Whatever the topic, an effective role-play helps to deepen your understanding of the people and events that change society.

Step 1: Research your role so that your role-play will accurately reflect the situation and people you portray.

Step 2: After finding the factual information you need, consider the emotional realm of the situation. How might the people you are portraying feel? How might they react to other people and events? When developing your character, be sure to avoid stereotypes and unrealistic characterization.

Step 3: Collect or make props and costumes to help you create a realistic role-play. Sketch a backdrop on a chalkboard or use an overhead projector or computer projection to make a temporary visual set. Extras, such as sound effects and music, will add to the effectiveness of your role-play.

Step 4: Whether your role-play is improvised or scripted, be sure to take time to rehearse. This will add to the confidence in your delivery.

◀ Students participate in a role-play in a classroom.

Step 5: Present your role-play. Be aware that staying in character, making smooth transitions between speaking roles, projecting your voice, and making appropriate eye contact and body movements will ensure that you have an attentive and appreciative audience.

Step 6: Debrief the role-play with your class. Give further information to the class about the situation and characters. Respond to any questions. Ask for feedback from other students and your teacher.

Step 7: Reflect on the process of creating your role-play as well as the actual presentation. What challenges did you face? What might you change for a future performance? What do you think went well?

Simulations

A simulation is similar to a role-play in that it requires that you research, rehearse, and maintain a dramatic persona and scene. It differs from a role-play in that you usually have to sustain an assigned character over an extended period of time, perhaps even for an entire class period. You also have to interact with others in the class without the assistance of a completely prepared script or an extended rehearsal. Simulations are very challenging and are meant to recreate complex situations where many people must react collectively.

▶ In this simulation of a model UN Assembly, students are representing various countries.

The following are examples of civics simulations:

- political campaigns and elections
- municipal council meetings, town hall meetings, committee meetings
- criminal or civil trials
- mediations
- panels of experts
- direct action (political protest of various forms)
- conventions on human rights or the environment
- UN assemblies and other international meetings
- war crimes tribunals
- federal/provincial conferences

In a simulation, you must be comfortable and familiar enough with your assigned role to interact in a realistic manner with all other players. Preparation is the key to a successful simulation. Parts of a simulation should be scripted (speeches, preparation of key questions, and opening and closing statements). However, most of the simulation depends on you and your classmates' ability to respond effectively to a multitude of actions and statements. You can follow steps 1–7 of a role-play for a simulation.

Unit Conclusion

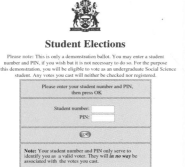

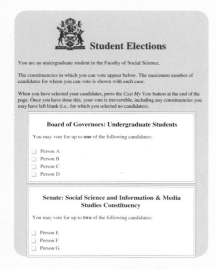

▲ These are sample ballots from a 1999 student election at the University of Western Ontario (London).

1. Why is it important that Canadians can amend their own Constitution without the approval of the British Parliament?

2. Why should a Canadian citizen be aware of the actions of the federal and provincial governments?

3. What are the possible consequences of

   a) people not fulfilling their citizenship responsibilities?

   b) people not using their citizenship rights?

4. What are some of the advantages and disadvantages of being able to amend the Constitution?

5. In 1999, the University of Western Ontario used the Internet to conduct a student election. What are some potential difficulties in using the Internet to hold federal and provincial elections?

6. Parts of the Canadian government (the governor general, the lieutenant governors, and the Senate) are not elected.

   a) Is this acceptable in a democracy?

   b) How would our political system be changed if these institutions were elected?

   c) Write a short, supported argument that justifies your point of view.

7. Imagine that you are a new immigrant to Canada. List five services you might require, and outline some of the ways the different levels of government could directly affect you.

8. If you were running for student council in your school, list three ways that you would try to get students to vote.

9. Prepare a brief report on an issue in your municipality. Write your report to answer who, what, when, where, and why?

10. Find out the name of the person who is

- governor general
- prime minister
- leader of the federal official opposition
- your federal MP
- lieutenant governor of your province
- premier of your province
- leader of the official opposition in your province
- leader of the third party in your province
- your MLA/MPP/MNA

11. Role-play one of the following events:

a) a political candidate planning his or her campaign with advisers

b) an immigrant's experience in Canada

c) a conflict based on the *Canadian Charter of Rights and Freedoms* (e.g., freedom of the press, mandatory retirement, or freedom of thought)

▲ Students role-play a political campaign.

The Active Citizen

Focus Questions

This unit explores these questions:

- *What kind of Canada do we want?*

- *What determines whether a person will participate in politics?*

- *How can individual Canadians actively challenge governments to make specific improvements to Canadians' lives?*

- *Who has the right to government information?*

- *Should we change the way we elect our governments in Canada?*

- *Why is Quebec's relationship with the rest of Canada so important?*

- *What changes have been made to improve the lives of Aboriginal peoples in Canada?*

What Is This Unit About?

From time to time, every citizen asks what Canada stands for and what we want it to be. We ask ourselves how we can change things and how we can get others to help us achieve these goals.

In a democracy, all citizens can share in decision making, mainly by electing politicians to represent their interests. Voting is a major responsibility of active citizens. Sometimes, when issues are complex and many people hold different points of view, it is difficult to decide what we want and how to go about getting it. Should the majority rule? Canada has many people who do not feel part of the majority. Some people may ask the following questions:

- Are our voting processes fair to all citizens?

- Can minority groups in Canada live comfortably within our democratic structure?

Québécois and Aboriginal peoples have historically been minorities in Canada. Since the 1960s, some significant issues have made Québécois and Aboriginal societies the focus of attention for all Canadians.

Key Terms

Aboriginal peoples

advance polls

assimilation

autonomy

boycott

First Nations

first past the post (FPTP)

interest group

Inuit

lobbyist

majority

Métis

non-status Indians

non-treaty Indians

plurality

political socialization

proportional representation (PR)

ratified

referendum

separatists

sovereignty

status Indians

treaty Indians

3.1 | Political Participation

Focus Question

- *What kind of Canada do we want?*

In 2005, the United Nations ranked Canada number five of the best countries in the world in which to live. This is not the first time the world community has recognized Canada. In fact, it was rated number one for more than a decade. Immigrants consistently rate Canada as one of the most desirable nations in which to live. Canada is one of a handful of nations whose citizens generally do not have large-scale problems obtaining food, shelter, or education.

Although Canada scored well on the United Nations list for income and education, it ranked much lower in areas such as child poverty. Canada has been criticized for its record on the environment, job creation, and the social and economic conditions of **Aboriginal peoples** living in Canada. Since we are such a rich nation, many ask why Canada cannot solve these social and economic problems. In addition, longstanding political differences between Quebec and the other nine provinces almost led to a breakup of Canada when Quebec citizens voted in a second **sovereignty** referendum in 1995.

Let's Discuss

Research the United Nations Human Development Index and list five reasons why Canada ranks so high on it.

Aboriginal peoples:
A collective term that refers to the three different groups of people—First Nations, Inuit, and Métis people in Canada; their ancestors were the indigenous or first peoples who inhabited North America.

sovereignty: Independence or nationhood; in Canada, Aboriginal or Quebec sovereignty is a goal shared by some, but not all, residents of Canada.

The United Nations Human Development Index, 2005

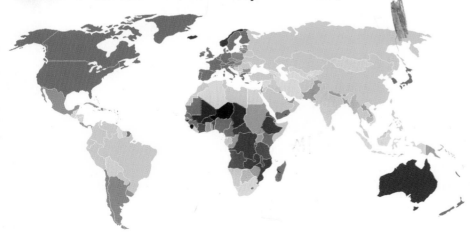

◄ The colours indicate the level of development, ranging from green for high to yellow/orange for medium, and red for low.

The Active Citizen

The active citizen is one who often questions the status quo—the way things are in his or her community or the wider society. This individual may have deeply held beliefs about a number of issues, or he or she may focus on a certain issue. For instance, everyone wants affordable health care with easy access to health professionals and good treatment when required. But health care is a complex subject. The active citizen who chooses to work for better services could work on several different aspects of the issue:

- hospital emergency services
- medical testing and treatment
- early childhood health
- cancer treatment
- AIDS treatment
- mental health
- smoking and teenagers
- the shortage of family physicians

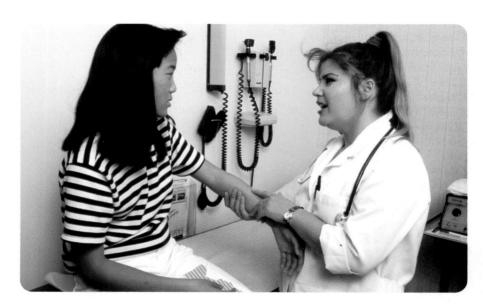

▶ This teen visits a doctor. In Ontario, the costs are covered by the Ontario Health Insurance Plan.

Often, people join groups or organizations that focus on one of these particular issues or another issue that they think is important.

Some citizens want to cut costs to taxpayers; others want expanded access to services in both cities and rural areas, particularly in remote parts of the north, even if this means additional costs to the taxpayer. Politicians have to respond to interest groups and to issues that have a major impact on the well-being of society.

Walkerton's Water

Active citizens interested in health care often take safe drinking water for granted. But in 2000, the issue of safe, clean water became a central topic in public discussion and debate. The water system in the town of Walkerton, Ontario, was polluted with E. coli, an infection resulting from bacteria. Seven residents died, and over 2000 were seriously sick simply from drinking their local water.

Before the Walkerton water treatment system became contaminated, safety measures had been reduced. Officials ignored warning signs and did not repair broken equipment. When the residents were finally told about the threat to their health, many people were already ill. Ontario Premier Mike Harris was criticized for cutting funding for water testing labs.

The news coverage of the problems in Walkerton increased public awareness of the importance of clean, safe water. In October 2002, Ontario passed the *Safe Water Act,* and everyone was assured that the problem was fixed. In October 2005, however, many of the 1700 Cree people on the Kashechewan reserve on James Bay, 400 km north of Timmins, were evacuated because their local water system was polluted with E. coli. The settlement had to be rebuilt at the cost of billions of dollars.

Questions

1. Research the Walkerton pollution tragedy and list three errors that led to the crisis.

2. How would you have reacted at the time? Pretend you are the following:

   a) a provincial politician

   b) an Ontario taxpayer

   c) a health care professional

   d) a citizen of Walkerton

   e) a member of the family of a victim

◀ This sign shows the outrage of people in Walkerton over the 2000 water pollution scandal.

Web Links

Walkerton's Water
To learn more about the decisions that contributed to the Walkerton tragedy, go to **www.nelson.com/civicsnow.**

"Vanishing Voter"
from *Civics Now DVD*.

Literacy Strategy

Skim the title and the Focus Question. What do you think will be the content of the section? Jot down some answers to the Focus Question before you read. Return to them afterward. Make connections between the topic and the world you live in to help you understand the concept.

Civics Now DVD

Voting Patterns

Focus Question

- *What determines whether a person will participate in politics?*

Several years ago, a government inquiry called the act of voting in an election the "single most important act of political participation in a modern democracy such as Canada." Why is this? How can simply voting be so important?

If the number of citizens voting is high, it indicates that there is a great amount of commitment and loyalty to Canada's political system. In other words, if many Canadians vote, we know that Canadian citizens are interested in the welfare of the nation.

If the number of citizens voting is low, it indicates that many citizens do not care about the political system that governs them. Elected representatives cannot claim that their decisions are fully supported when large numbers of citizens have not cast their ballots in an election.

International Voter Turnout, 1991-2000

Country	1991-1995	1996-2000	Average	Country	1991-1995	1996-2000	Average
Argentina	82%	78%	81%	Iceland	89%		89%
Australia	83%	82%	83%	Ireland	74%	67%	71%
Austria	78%		78%	Italy	92%	87%	90%
Belgium	84%		84%	Luxembourg	60%		60%
Bolivia	50%	62%	56%	Mexico	58%	57%	58%
Brazil	77%		77%	Netherlands	75%		75%
Canada	64%	56%	60%	Norway	74%	77%	76%
Chile	82%		82%	Peru	58%		58%
Colombia	28%	40%	32%	Portugal	79%		79%
Denmark	82%	83%	83%	Spain	77%	81%	79%
Dominican Republic	31%	62%	47%	Sweden	84%		84%
				Switzerland	38%		38%
Ecuador	66%	58%	61%	Thailand	61%	65%	62%
Finland	71%		71%	Turkey	80%		80%
France	61%	60%	61%	United Kingdom	75%	69%	72%
Germany	72%		72%				
Greece	86%	84%	85%	United States	47%	44%	45%
Guatemala	24%		24%	Venezuela	50%		50%

Voting Problems

Canada's voter turnout figure of 60 percent is lower than most other democracies on the list on page 84 except for the United States (45 percent). When four out of ten citizens do not vote, it means that a minority of citizens elects most Canadian governments.

An increase to 80 percent would be a dramatic improvement for Canada and would allow Canada to match the average turnout rates of other democracies such as Australia or Sweden. Before we can figure out how to get 20 percent more citizens out to vote, we have to understand why so many Canadians do not vote. Below are reasons that researchers found for Canadians deciding not to vote.

Voter Turnout at Canada's Federal Elections, 1979–2003

Year	Percent Turnout
1979	76%
1980	69%
1984	75%
1988	76%
1993	70%
1997	67%
2000	61%
2003	60%

Reasons for Not Voting

Reason	% of All Respondents	% of Non-Voters
Politicians and Political Institutions		
Politicians (negative image by the public)	26.2	24.9
Government (negative image by the public)	13.0	16.0
Candidates (negative image by the public)	11.7	12.4
Political parties (negative image by the public)	6.3	6.2
Issues (negative public attitudes)	5.5	4.2
Leaders (negative image by the public)	3.3	2.3
Electoral system (negative image by the public)	1.0	0.5
Election administration (problems)	1.0	1.2
	68.0	**67.7**

Reason	% of All Respondents	% of Non-Voters
Meaninglessness		
Meaninglessness of participation	15.7	14.5
Lack of competition	14.0	8.6
Regional discontent	2.8	1.8
	32.5	**24.9**
Public Apathy		
Apathy and lack of interest	22.7	24.2
Turned attention elsewhere	5.1	5.8
Lack of knowledge, information	4.3	5.0
Cynicism	4.0	3.4
Youth not voting	3.1	1.9
	39.2	**40.3**
Other	3.1	5.0
Do not know	1.4	2.5

The Teen Voter

As the table below clearly shows, younger citizens do not vote. In fact, according to Elections Canada statistics, less than one-quarter of citizens aged 18 to 20 voted in the 2000 election.

Age and Voting Turnout (Federal Election, 2000)

Ages (years)	Voted (%)	Did Not Vote (%)
18-20	22.4	77.6
21-24	27.5	72.5
25-29	38.2	61.8
30-37	54.2	45.8
38-47	66.2	33.8
48-57	76.4	23.6
58-67	80.4	19.6
68+	83.3	16.7
Total	**61.3**	**38.7**

Why do younger citizens have lower voter turnout rates than older citizens?

- Do younger people know less about the voting process?
- Are students attending college or university far from home unaware of elections or confused about how to get on the voters' list?
- Have younger people not developed a strong interest in politics yet?

Our challenge is to raise the level of voting by all citizens, regardless of age.

▲ These students are participating in a class election. This encourages teens to become active citizen voters after they turn 18.

Let's Discuss

List three cases from your personal experience in which you had to vote on something (for example, high school student council; school team or group; community organizations). Did you participate in the voting? Why or why not?

Increasing the Turnout

Several countries make voting compulsory for their citizens, that is, citizens are required by law to vote. Australia established compulsory voting in 1911. In Australia, non-voters pay a small penalty if their excuse is not accepted by a special board. Undoubtedly, penalties "persuade" some citizens who might not vote voluntarily to cast a ballot on election day. However, most democracies do not use this method

Ideas to Get More People Voting

When we study other reasons for not voting, we find that some Canadians are away on election day, have not been enumerated, or are sick. The Royal Commission on Electoral Reform came up with these suggestions for improving the turnout rate:

Advance Polls

Advance polls (the poll is the place you go to vote) allows citizens to vote on several designated days before election day if they will be away on the actual day of the election. To help the most voters, it is best to allow several weeks for advance voting.

Mail-in Voting

Allow postal voting, whereby voters would apply for a ballot, sign a declaration stating they were unable to vote on election day, and mail the ballot before election day.

Special Needs Assistance

Expand the opportunities for assisting voters with special needs, for visually impaired citizens, and for citizens with language or other challenges. One idea is to include a picture of each candidate on the ballot.

Sunday Voting

Sunday voting might encourage more people to vote. By law, employers must give employees time off work to vote, but many find that they have to squeeze voting into the time between the end of the workday and 8:00 or 8:30 P.M. when the polls close. Most people don't work on Sunday. For those who do work, voting could take place in advance, postal, or evening polls. Several European democracies have Sunday voting, and they also have higher voter turnouts.

Let's Discuss

Over 30 countries around the world have passed laws to make voting required for all citizens. State an argument for compulsory voting and one against it. Should we have compulsory voting in Canada?

Literacy Strategy

Before reading, jot down some ideas you may have to help you with the assignments in **Let's Discuss.** Read the page and think about how you plan to respond to the assignments. After reading, plan your response to the assignments. Note your ideas on paper, make judgments, and justify them to yourself. Preparing the assignments in this way helps you organize your thoughts and ensures that you don't forget important points.

Let's Discuss

Divide into groups and take one of the four suggestions about improving the turnout rate. Debate the pros and cons of advance polls, mail-in voting, special needs assistance, and Sunday voting. Share your conclusions with the class.

Your Political Self

These suggestions might help increase Canada's voting turnout rate, but would they get it to the 80 percent goal we mentioned earlier? Major reasons for not voting are that some citizens are simply not interested in the election outcome and some do not believe that voting is an important citizen responsibility. Before we can change these attitudes, we have to understand why citizens feel negatively about politics and voting.

Learning Political Beliefs

The term **political socialization** describes how we learn our political beliefs. We form our attitudes about society and our role in it early in life. Young children learn attitudes about citizenship and politics from their families and their schools. For example, primary school teachers constantly talk about the importance of sharing and helping classmates. To instill a respect for authority, police officers or firefighters often visit elementary classrooms.

Many students see these authority figures positively. They also may know about Canada's symbols, such as the national anthem and the Canadian flag. Students often accept class and school rules, even though they do not always obey them. At an early age, students learn and absorb many of the ideas of good citizenship that they apply to the larger community as they get older.

As you move into your teenage years, other forces help you develop your "political self."

- If you are involved in clubs, teams, scouting, cadets, or religious groups, these groups reinforce the beliefs about participation, leadership, and majority rule that are at the heart of politics.

- If your family reaches decisions in a democratic way and you are encouraged to make decisions for yourself, you are adopting these attitudes.

- At the same time, your parents' political beliefs can influence your own support for a political party or politician.

- By the time you reach voting age, your political self is well on its way to being fully formed.

Students who have bad experiences growing up may develop a hostile attitude toward authority figures, which could include politicians and the electoral system. This could be a reason why they do not vote.

▲ Former Toronto Chief of Police Julian Fantino talks to a class of elementary school children. This encourages children to respect authority.

Lowering the Voting Age to 16

"It might be a good idea to lower the voting age. But, it could be a bad idea, too, because, at 16, one is more easily influenced. Not everyone has made a choice. However, my mind is made up. I can't wait to vote, but lowering the voting age would be risky. Voting must be personal and not influenced by anyone."

"No. We must be given time to mature, gain experience, listen, read, and see. At age 16, we are still influenced by our parents and friends."

"As students, we learn about the voting process and civic responsibility in civics class. If we pass the civics course, shouldn't we then be allowed to vote?"

Questions

1. List three reasons why the voting age should be lowered to 16. List three reasons why it should not. Share these with the class.
2. List two ways that politicians could appeal to the teenage voter.
3. What kind of information would you need to make an intelligent decision at voting time?

▶ These young people are learning the responsibilities of active citizenship by voting in a school election.

⟷ Check Your Understanding

1. List the reasons most commonly given by people for not voting.
2. How might the level of voter participation be increased?
3. What is the ideal age to be eligible to vote in Canada? Justify your answer.

3.2 | Interest Groups

Focus Question

- *How can individual Canadians actively challenge governments to make specific improvements to Canadians' lives?*

boycott: An effort by a group to refuse to deal with a person or organization to protest its actions.

interest group: A group of people that represents a particular occupation or common goal and influences governments to pass laws favouring these goals.

Voting in an election is not the only way to make changes in a democracy. Citizens have used protests and marches, letter writing and petitions, or **boycotts** to influence their elected representatives. Another way to bring about change is to form or join an **interest group.**

The Coalition to End Child Poverty is an interest group with a common goal. The Canadian Medical Association is an influential professional interest group that represents doctors. There are thousands of similar groups. Some have existed for years and have permanent headquarters and paid staff, while others last for only a short time before disbanding. How do these groups operate?

▲ One way students can make a difference is by signing petitions.

Methods of Interest Groups

- meeting with cabinet ministers and civil servants to press their case
- having **lobbyists** attend parliamentary committees about legislation affecting them
- paying for ads on television, radio, and in newspapers
- using Web sites to educate the public about their issues
- distributing pamphlets
- setting up information tables at local events
- contacting local organizations to offer speakers
- writing letters to newspapers

lobbyist: A registered representative of a company or interest group who tries to influence government policy.

Difference

Matthew Coon Come

Matthew Coon Come was one of the leaders of the successful protest against the Quebec government's plans to build another enormous hydroelectric project in the middle of Cree lands, near James Bay in Quebec.

Born in 1956 on his parent's trapline near Mistassini, Quebec, Coon Come did not see a white person until he was six years old. At a young age, Coon Come was soon recognized for his intelligence and leadership skills. He served two terms as Chief of the Mistassini First Nation. Before he left to join his father on the family trapline, Coon Come had negotiated many improvements in his community: a new arena, an adult education centre, a band administrative office, health facilities, and upgraded housing.

In 1987, he was elected grand chief and chairman of the Grand Council of the Cree of Quebec. He held that post for 12 years. In July 2000, he was elected national chief of the Assembly of First Nations and organized the protest against the Hydro-Québec project that would have flooded many hectares of Cree lands.

Coon Come took the bold step of going to the United Nations. He addressed the UN General Assembly in August 2001 about the plight of Aboriginal people in Canada. His public protests in New York made the Cree cause front-page news. U.S. utility companies were forced to back away from signing new contracts with Hydro-Québec for the power that would come from the new project. The Cree lands were saved from flooding.

Questions

1. How did Coon Come use the media to get his message to the American public?
2. In your opinion, should citizens take their concerns about Canada to authorities outside of the country?

◄ Cree Chief Matthew Coon Come testifies at a hearing to stop the construction of a new power project that would have flooded large areas of Cree land in Northern Quebec.

"The Good Fight"
from *Civics Now DVD*.

▲ No smoking signs can be seen in many public places in Ontario.

Civics Now DVD

"Anti-Smoking"
from *Civics Now DVD*.

Pros and Cons of Interest Groups

Many Canadians would applaud the Cree victory over the construction of a new power project. This is a positive example of interest groups.

But what about the interest groups we might not support? For example, the Canadian Tobacco Manufacturers Council (CTMC) is a lobby group representing the tobacco industry. It tries to disprove any claims by anti-smoking groups such as the Canadian Cancer Society or the Canadian Medical Association. The CTMC believes that tobacco is a legal product and, as such, it should be available to any adult who wishes to buy it. The anti-smoking groups state that smoking is harmful to your health, and tobacco is addictive.

Opponents of interest groups say that some of these groups have too much influence on government. We elect representatives to Parliament to pass laws that benefit all of us, while interest groups promote goals that all citizens do not share. Critics argue that interest groups present one-sided arguments and facts to support their cases. Defenders of interest groups point out that our elected representatives require information to draft laws. A group that specializes in a specific area can provide technical and complicated data to help our elected representatives.

↔ Check Your Understanding

1. Research interest groups. List three interest groups and what or whom they represent. What makes each an interest group?

2. In a sentence or two, define the purpose of each interest group you found in question 1.

3. Give three reasons to support interest groups and three reasons to oppose them.

Let's Discuss

Are interest groups a benefit or a threat to democracy? Discuss with the class. Be prepared to defend your response.

3.3 | Government Accountability

Focus Question

- *Who has the right to government information?*

In order to learn more about the issues that concern them, citizens who want change often need information that usually only government departments can provide.

In 1985, Canada passed the *Access to Information Act,* which gives any citizen the right to obtain copies of federal government records. Each province has similar legislation. These records include an extensive list—everything from letters and reports to computer files. The only exceptions are documents that could injure Canada's military security, international relations, or economy. Information about individuals, such as health or tax records, cannot be disclosed without their consent.

Literacy Strategy

Skim the title and the Focus Question, and think about the **Let's Discuss** assignment before you read. As you read, consider how you will answer the discussion question and justify your answer.

Let's Discuss

Why can't every Canadian citizen see every government record? After all, we are citizens and taxpayers. Discuss in small groups. Be prepared to defend your opinion.

▲ The federal and provincial governments keep extensive records like these on all citizens and organizations in the country or province.

Access Rights

Citizens' access to information is now regarded as a basic democratic right. Governments are not permitted to hide information that might prove embarrassing to them. Although some types of information (as noted above) are exempt from release, citizens can call upon the information commissioner if government departments do not answer a request for information. Citizens and interest groups have a rich resource when they need information.

Using Information Access

Let's look at an example of how a citizen interest group could use such information. Your local environmental group is worried that a foreign company has plans to buy local water and sell it to foreign governments and businesses. Your municipal government tells you that the federal government deals with all exports, so this is not their problem. Your group requests information from the federal government under the *Access to Information Act,* and they do not reply.

So, your group goes to the information commissioner. This person looks into problems citizens might have obtaining information. In this case, the information commissioner criticizes the government for not providing information to your group. Finally, you receive the information and are able to organize public protests to stop the sale of our water.

▲ Canada has an abundant supply of fresh water, such as this lake in Muskoka. Many citizens are worried about plans to sell our water.

Let's Discuss

Have you or someone you know been involved in a public project, such as this protest against water sales? If so, explain to the class what you did.

Web Links

The Privacy Commissioner
To learn more about the privacy commissioner's job go to **www.nelson.com/civicsnow.**

Maude Barlow

The sale of Canada's fresh water has long been a concern for Maude Barlow. She is one of Canada's best-known citizen activists. She is chairperson of the 100 000-member Council of Canadians. She founded that organization in 1985 to preserve Canadian independence. Barlow has fought public campaigns against the proposed selling of Canadian water to foreign buyers, among many other issues. A polished speaker, Maude Barlow is an excellent debater. She is also the author of a dozen books on social and political issues, including *Blue Water: The Fight to Stop Corporate Theft of the World's Water.*

Questions

1. The selling of Canadian water to the United States and others is an idea that is hotly debated. List three pros and three cons of selling Canadian water.

2. Maude Barlow's Council of Canadians wants to keep Canada independent. How will not selling our water keep us independent?

Literacy Strategy

After reading the feature, think about how you can make connections between what you have learned and the world around you. Use your prior knowledge about people and events you know.

▲ Maude Barlow is a well-known Canadian citizen activist.

Web Links

Maude Barlow and the Council of Canadians
To learn more about the Council of Canadians and Maude Barlow, go to **www.nelson.com/civicsnow.**

The Issue of Privacy

Governments have a huge amount of information in their files and computer databases about a citizen over a lifetime:
- census data (e.g., birth records)
- school records
- student-loan applications
- health records
- tax records
- police records and data
- employment insurance
- pensions
- government employment records
- security clearances
- immigration details

Put these details together and they can draw a surprisingly revealing picture of a citizen—too revealing if another person gained access to that information. In 1983, the government passed the *Privacy Act,* which gives any Canadian the right to examine information held about her or him and to correct any errors in the details.

Computers and the Internet have changed the way we live. They have also changed the way we look at privacy. To help address modern privacy concerns, the government passed the *Personal Information Protection and Electronic Documents Act* (PIPEDA) in 2000. This Act governs how all organizations may use the information that individuals provide to them.

Police and national security officials, however, worry that criminals and terrorists will also be able to communicate in complete privacy and be safe from investigators. They have suggested that all passwords be registered with them, as a kind of electronic master key to locked information.

Questions

1. List two situations when police should be able to access database files, such as criminal records of young people.

2. People claim that street cameras mounted at intersections help catch drivers who fail to stop or otherwise break the law. List two pros and two cons of these street cameras.

3. Which is more important in our society—privacy or safety? Prepare an answer, giving at least two good reasons for your position.

▲ The *Privacy Act* allows all citizens to examine and correct government information about themselves.

Referendums

A **referendum** is a process that allows every citizen a say on some question of importance to a nation or community by means of a direct vote. In Canada, the federal government rarely uses referendums, but, from time to time, they are used for serious issues.

An important referendum was held in 1992, when the federal government of Canada proposed changing the Constitution. Known as the Charlottetown Accord, it was supported by federal, provincial, and territorial governments, as well as most Aboriginal leaders. The government did not get the results it had hoped for, and the Canadian people defeated the plans to change the Constitution.

▲ Pro-unity supporters rally during the 1995 Referendum on Quebec separation from Canada.

Quebec has held two referendums, in 1980 and 1995, on the issue of the separation of Quebec from Canada. In both votes, the "No" side won, but the margin was extremely close in 1995. These two referendums were important for all Canadians. The referendums suggested other questions:

- Could a majority of voters in one province decide to leave Canada, splitting the country in two?

- What would happen to those who opposed separation who lived within Quebec?

- Did the voters really understand the referendum question being asked?

- Did Canadians really want their country to break up?

Quebec Referendum Results

Year	YES	NO
1980	40.4%	59.6%
1995	49.4%	50.6%

Opponents of Referendums

People who are against referendums point out that laws and issues are complex, but referendums usually require a straight "yes" or "no" answer. That means they oversimplify and even misrepresent the problem. Few citizens have the time to make knowledgeable choices about the issues involved. We elect politicians to do that for us, and, depending on how good a job they do, we vote them in or out in the next election. Most democracies seldom use referendums and instead rely on their elected representatives to make laws and decide on actions.

Citizens have other ways to make their wishes known to politicians:

- lobbying by interest groups
- letter and e-mail writing
- advertising, signs
- petitions
- protests
- text messaging
- blogs

Let's Discuss

If elected in Quebec, should the Parti Québécois hold another referendum on the separation of Quebec from Canada? Is it right that Canadians outside of Quebec were excluded from voting in both referendums? Explain.

▲ These young people are using signs to make their opinions on certain issues known to politicians.

A New Voting System for Canada?

Focus Question

- *Should we change the way we elect our governments in Canada?*

Setting Election Dates

In federal elections in Canada, the governing party can choose the date for an election any time within its five-year term. But in the United States, election dates are fixed to specific terms: four years for the president, six years for senators, and two years for Members of Congress. Recently, both Ontario and British Columbia announced fixed election dates every four years for future elections. When these announcements were made, both provinces had elected majority governments.

Electing Representatives

Some Canadians believe that our method of electing governments needs a radical change. They favour a system called **proportional representation (PR)** to replace our present system, which is called **first past the post (FPTP)**. To see how both systems work, let's consider an example from a school election.

Suppose a school has 1000 students. They vote for one of four candidates for student council president. The results in this election are as follows:

Student Candidate	Votes Received
Deng	350
Blair	300
Cristina	200
Ainsley	150
Total	1000

Under the first-past-the-post system, Deng wins. He has more votes than any of the four candidates. But he does not have the support of a majority of students. In fact, 650 students

proportional representation (PR): An electoral system that distributes seats according to the percentage of the total votes received by each party.

first past the post (FPTP): An electoral system in which the candidate receiving more votes than any other wins a seat in government.

plurality: The election result where one candidate receives more votes than any other, but less than 50 percent of the total votes.

majority: Most people; an election in which one candidate receives more than 50 percent of the total number of votes.

First Past the Post

Party	Percentage of Vote	Number of Seats
A	35%	155
B	30%	118
C	20%	25
D	15%	10

(or 65 percent of the student body) did not vote for Deng. He has a **plurality** of votes (more than any other candidate), but not a **majority** (51 percent or more of the total number of votes). In an election for a single position such as this, it's difficult to see how any other system could replace it.

Canadian Federal Elections

In Canadian elections, we often have several candidates running in every one of the 308 ridings in Canada. Each candidate represents one of a dozen or so official political parties. Just as in our student election, a winning candidate rarely gathers more than 50 percent of the votes cast in a riding. So a party that wins 155 ridings can form a majority government.

Suppose Party A wins 155 ridings, with an average of 35 percent of the votes cast, just as Deng won in the student election. On a national level, Party A forms a majority government—but it has the support of only approximately 35 percent of voters, not a majority. This, to supporters of proportional representation (PR), is the unfairness of first past the post (FPTP).

▲ This is the House of Commons in session. All members are elected through a first-past-the-post system.

The 1999 Ontario Election: A Fair and Democratic Result?

"Is the glass half empty or half full? The popular vote (Progressive Conservative, 45.1 percent; Liberal, 38.9 percent; NDP, 12.6 percent) says that 54.9 percent of Ontarians voted against the Harris Conservatives. Well, then, doesn't it follow that 61.1 percent voted anti-Liberal and 87.4 percent voted anti-NDP?"

"Once again, the minority (45.1 percent) is going to dictate the lives of the majority (54.9 percent). Doesn't democracy mean carrying out the will of the majority of the people (50 percent plus one)? In this election, almost 20 of the Progressive Conservative Party's 59 seats were won with less than half the votes in those ridings. Not enough ridings had a majority to form a majority government. In Europe, voters can make a second choice so that a second ballot will give a clear winner. Until we do this, don't tell me we live in a democracy."

▲ Premier Mike Harris won the 1999 Ontario provincial election. He got less than half of all votes but won a majority in the legislature, an example of the first-past-the-post system.

Questions

1. In Canadian federal and provincial elections, the candidate with more votes than any other wins. This is known as the first-past-the-post system. List three pros and three cons of this system.
2. Create a chart listing three pros and three cons of proportional representation.
3. What is your opinion regarding first-past-the-post and proportional systems? Give two reasons for your opinion.

A Proportional System

Proportional representation could make elections fairer by distributing seats on the basis of the percentage of the total vote that each party receives. As the chart on the right shows, Party A does not have a majority of the seats. It would have to form an alliance with another party, such as Party B or Party C, to get a total of over 155 seats and form a working coalition government.

Several European governments have proportional representation. Systems for dividing the seats among the candidates vary. Some PR systems have each party draw up a list of candidates ready to take office. In each riding, electors vote for a party, not a person. When the results are totalled, each party selects the candidates to represent it in Parliament from its list.

Proportional Representation

Party	Percentage of Vote	Number of Seats
A	35%	108
B	30%	92
C	20%	62
D	15%	46

Supporters of proportional representation argue that this system reflects the wishes of the voters more fairly. In our example, the percentage of seats each party receives exactly matches the percentage of total votes it receives. A first-past-the-post system, in contrast, often gives a majority of the seats to a party that did not receive a majority of total votes.

Those against proportional representation argue that it too often results in minority governments that find it hard to make decisions. For example, if Parties A and B form such a government, they may have such different points of view that any action becomes difficult and time-consuming.

Process of Elimination

Political parties choose their leaders only when an absolute majority—over half—of the voting delegates approve the choice. If the leading candidate does not have 51 percent of the votes, the candidate with the smallest number of votes is dropped from the ballot. Then another round of voting occurs. Sometimes two, three, four, or more ballots are held before a winner is declared.

Sometimes a candidate will try to prevent the front-runner from winning by making a deal to support a runner-up. Then that candidate personally withdraws from the race and asks her or his supporters to support the candidate she or he endorsed. Voters must then make a clear choice. Eventually a clear winner is named.

▲ Paul Martin won the Liberal leadership convention in November 2003, with over 50 percent of the votes.

↔ Check Your Understanding

1. How does the *Access to Information Act* ensure that some of the most basic elements of democracy are available and used in Canada?

2. Should referendums continue to be used in Canada in order to gage the public's opinions on how the government should operate?

3. Explain the two methods for electing governments in Canada.

4. Which system of elections do you feel we should use in Canada? Provide two or three arguments to support your opinion.

3.4 Quebec and Citizenship

Focus Question

- *Why is Quebec's relationship with the rest of Canada so important?*

On October 30, 1995, Canadians gathered anxiously around their television sets. They awaited the results of a vote that would determine the future of their country. The people of Quebec were deciding whether they would stay in Canada or leave it.

The referendum was emotional and dramatic. The Yes side—the forces for Quebec independence—were first led by Quebec Premier Jacques Parizeau. But when polls showed that the No side was well ahead, the Yes side decided to gamble: they changed leaders. Lucien Bouchard, the leader of the Bloc Québécois, the federal arm of the Quebec independence movement, took over leadership of the Yes forces. Bouchard was an outstanding speaker and an inspiring leader. Quebeckers began to rally behind him and the Yes forces. Would they take the final step and decide to split the nation?

The No side warned of economic disaster if Quebec separated from Canada. But many citizens of Quebec, especially younger ones, were willing to take a chance. In the days before the October 30 vote, the Yes and No sides appeared to be tied. Federalist forces from across Canada rallied in Montreal in the days before the vote. A huge demonstration urged Quebeckers to vote against separation. Over the weekend, the future of Canada appeared to be hanging in the balance.

When the referendum vote occurred two days later, it could not have been closer: 50.6 percent voted No; 49.4 percent voted Yes. Quebec would stay in Canada—but the Yes side vowed to try again.

Let's Discuss

According to the 1995 Referendum results, nearly half of Quebec citizens wanted independence from Canada. Why do you think so many voted for independence? Explain your answer.

▲ Lucien Bouchard led the Yes forces during the 1995 Referendum.

Civics Now DVD

"The Great Divide" from *Civics Now DVD*.

Quebec: Federalism or Separatism

The French and English have a long history of "sharing" Canada. They fought each other over the fur trade and other issues, until the British Empire conquered the French Empire in the middle of the 18th century. French-speaking and English-speaking Canadians have since agreed to disagree on many things.

The Quiet Revolution

In 1960, a new Liberal government, led by Jean Lesage, took power and set about modernizing the province. This Quiet Revolution changed Quebec by getting French-speaking citizens involved in business and government. Their slogan was "Masters of our own house" *(Maîtres chez nous)* and "Things must change" *(Il faut que ça change)*. The new government took over education from the church and spent millions on new schools and colleges. It also took over all the private hydroelectric companies and formed one of the largest government-owned electrical companies in the world—Hydro-Québec. Profits from this huge resource flowed to the government, not to private investors. French-Canadian engineers built the new hydro dams. Quebec was on the move—confident and modern.

▲ Premier Jean Lesage was a key player in the Quiet Revolution.

Timeline: French-English Relations

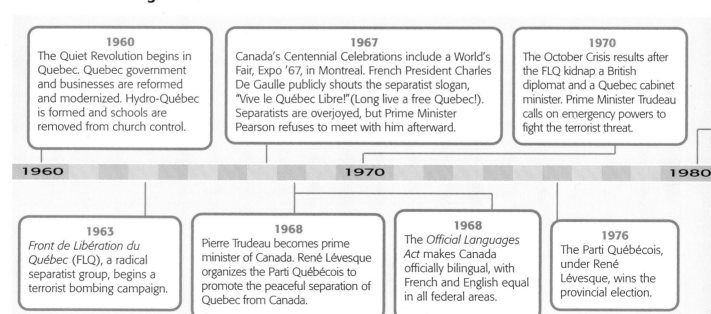

1960
The Quiet Revolution begins in Quebec. Quebec government and businesses are reformed and modernized. Hydro-Québec is formed and schools are removed from church control.

1967
Canada's Centennial Celebrations include a World's Fair, Expo '67, in Montreal. French President Charles De Gaulle publicly shouts the separatist slogan, "Vive le Québec Libre!" (Long live a free Quebec!). Separatists are overjoyed, but Prime Minister Pearson refuses to meet with him afterward.

1970
The October Crisis results after the FLQ kidnap a British diplomat and a Quebec cabinet minister. Prime Minister Trudeau calls on emergency powers to fight the terrorist threat.

1960   **1970**   **1980**

1963
Front de Libération du Québec (FLQ), a radical separatist group, begins a terrorist bombing campaign.

1968
Pierre Trudeau becomes prime minister of Canada. René Lévesque organizes the Parti Québécois to promote the peaceful separation of Quebec from Canada.

1968
The *Official Languages Act* makes Canada officially bilingual, with French and English equal in all federal areas.

1976
The Parti Québécois, under René Lévesque, wins the provincial election.

The "Three Wise Men"

At the federal level, in the mid-1960s, Prime Minister Lester Pearson looked for bright and energetic people to renew the Canadian government, just as they were doing in Quebec. He also reached out to the Quebecois leaders and brought in "Three Wise Men"—the young and popular Gérard Pelletier, Jean Marchand, and Pierre Trudeau—from Quebec. He also attracted Jean Chrétien to Ottawa. (Both Trudeau and Chrétien went on to become prime ministers of Canada.) These Quebec politicians were federalists who wanted a strong federal government in Ottawa that would promote language rights and equality for both official language groups.

◀ Jean Marchand, Pierre Trudeau, and Gérard Pelletier (left to right) were known as the "Three Wise Men."

1980
Quebec holds a referendum on independence from Canada. Lévesque's "Yes" side wins 40 percent of the vote, while Trudeau's "No" side wins 60 percent of the vote.

1990
The Meech Lake Accord was created to bring Quebec to sign the Constitution. It fails to pass as Manitoba and Newfoundland reject it.

1995
The second referendum on Quebec separation is narrowly defeated. The Canadian nationalists win a very slim majority (50.6 percent to 49.4 percent).

1998
The Parti Québécois wins the provincial election in Quebec.

1990 **2000**

1982
Quebec refuses to sign the Canadian Constitution.

1992
The Charlottetown Accord, designed to make the Canadian Constitution easier to change and give more power to the provinces, is defeated in a national referendum. Brian Mulroney resigns as prime minister shortly afterward.

2003
The Quebec Liberal Party, under Jean Charest, wins the provincial election. Paul Martin, of the federal Liberal Party, wins a minority election and becomes prime minister of Canada.

The October Crisis

Some Quebeckers called for a radical approach. The separatists wanted Quebec to split completely from Canada and become a separate nation. There were many groups of separatists. Some believed that violent revolution was necessary to win Quebec independence. One of the violent groups, the *Front de Libération du Québec* (FLQ), used terrorist tactics, starting with planting bombs in the cities, to try to force change. In October 1970, they kidnapped a British trade official and the Quebec deputy premier, Pierre Laporte. When they killed Laporte, Prime Minister Trudeau placed Canada under emergency law, known as the *War Measures Act*. This act had only been used twice before, during the first and second world wars. It greatly restricted civil rights. Many suspects were jailed and held without trial until the terrorists were arrested or fled the country. Separatism lost some of its energy because of the crisis, but many Quebeckers resented the use of the *War Measures Act* against their province.

separatists: Individuals who support the separation of a province from the nation; in Canada, there has been a separatist movement in Quebec since the 1960s.

▲ Prime Minister Trudeau leaves an emergency meeting of Parliament after placing Canada under the *War Measures Act.*

▲ When the media asked Prime Minister Trudeau how far he was prepared to go after activating the *War Measures Act,* he replied, "Just watch me."

Trudeau and the Separatists

Prime Minister Trudeau had entered federal politics with one major aim: to help French Canadians to feel as if they belonged in Canada as full citizens. He believed that Canada's federal system could protect the French-Canadian language and culture. As a vigorous opponent of separatism, Trudeau gained wide support throughout English Canada. He appeared to be the leader who could keep Quebec within the Canadian Confederation.

Official Bilingualism

Trudeau wanted French Canadians to feel welcome anywhere they travelled or lived in Canada. In 1968, the Trudeau government made Canada officially bilingual. That meant that all federal government services—airports, post offices, employment bureaus—would be made available in both French and English. Thousands of federal civil servants had to take instruction in French (or English) language. The civil service would become bilingual and serve Canadian citizens in both official languages. Labels and instructions on consumer goods had to be written in both languages. The provinces were prodded to follow suit. New Brunswick became the only Canadian province to declare itself officially bilingual. All these efforts, Trudeau believed, would restore Quebec's faith in the goodwill of English Canada toward French Canadians.

The Separatist Movement

René Lévesque disagreed with Trudeau's federalism. Lévesque's vision was of a separate Quebec state that would promote French language and culture ahead of English. So, in 1968, René Lévesque formed the separatist Parti Québécois (PQ). Within a few years, the PQ won 30 percent of the vote in the provincial election. In 1976, it won the election and became the official government of Quebec. It promised a referendum on independence for Quebec. The rest of Canada was anxious, frightened, and confused over separatism's attraction for Quebeckers. Prime Minister Trudeau was a French Canadian himself, and he was determined to keep Quebec in Confederation.

The Referendum

In 1980, however, Quebec held its referendum. Premier René Lévesque softened his position on outright independent nationhood for Quebec. He asked Quebeckers to vote Yes or No on whether Quebec should negotiate for political independence—with economic association with Canada. By a margin of over six out of ten, Quebeckers voted "No." Trudeau's federalist strategy had won. Canada appeared to be holding together.

But most young Quebeckers had voted "Yes." The Parti Québécois would wait for another chance at a referendum. Young Quebeckers would influence their children to support Quebec's independence. Next time, the Parti Québécois believed, they would win. They did try again 15 years later—in 1995—and almost succeeded. Will they succeed next time?

▲ It is the law to have both English and French on all labels and instructions on consumer goods.

▲ René Lévesque speaks after the 1980 Referendum on separatism.

Let's Discuss

In 1980, Prime Minister Trudeau stated, "It would be a crime against humanity if Canada were to break up." Do you agree with Trudeau's opinion? Explain. Consider the example Canada presents to the rest of the world.

Web Links

The *Charter of Rights and Freedoms*

To learn more about the *Canadian Charter of Rights and Freedoms,* go to **www.nelson.com/civicsnow.**

▲ Prime Minister Brian Mulroney is shown here with Newfoundland Premier Clyde Wells (left) after a meeting on the Meech Lake Accord.

Citizenship and the Constitution

Prime Minister Trudeau had promised to change the Canadian Constitution to accommodate Quebec if the "No" side won. It did, and he set about creating a new constitution. Among those changes was a new *Canadian Charter of Rights and Freedoms*. At a conference in 1981, Trudeau and the ten provincial premiers seemed to agree about the *Charter* and other parts of the Constitution. But when it came time to sign the new *Constitution Act* the following year, Quebec refused. Quebec was opposed mainly because the *Act* did not give Quebec special status. It treated Quebec as merely another province of Canada. The *Constitution Act* and the *Charter* became law in Canada, without Quebec's signature. (See Unit 2 for more information about the Constitution and the *Charter*.)

Constitutional Reform and Beyond

In 1984, the new prime minister, Brian Mulroney, was determined to get Quebec to sign onto the Constitution. Within three years, he and the ten premiers had an agreement. The Meech Lake Accord included special provisions for Quebec, such as recognizing it as a "distinct society." All ten provincial governments had to formally agree to the Accord by June 1990. When Newfoundland and Manitoba failed to do so in time, the Accord failed.

Mulroney was not prepared to give up. The federal and provincial governments and other organizations continued to discuss constitutional reform. The result was the Charlottetown Accord in August 1992. All parties agreed that the proposals be presented for the citizens of Canada in a national referendum in October of that year. The result was close, but 54.4 percent voted against the Accord. That final defeat seemed to end Canadians' desire for constitutional reform.

↔ Check Your Understanding

1. a) Make a chart with two headings: "Canada's Leadership" and "Quebec's Leadership."

    b) In the chart, list the leaders and the dates that they held power in Canada and Quebec.

    c) Decide on the four most significant issues between 1960 and 2005 that affected Canada's relationship with Quebec. Enter those issues in the appropriate place on your chart.

    d) Record the reasons for your choices and be prepared to share your ideas with your class.

2. Do you think francophone Quebeckers have a stronger sense of identity with their province than other Canadians have with theirs? Give examples in your explanation of your answer.

3.5 | Aboriginal Citizens

Focus Question

- *What changes have been made to improve the lives of Aboriginal peoples in Canada?*

Aboriginal Diversity

Long before Europeans "found" Canada and began colonizing North America, Aboriginal peoples—of many different nations, languages, and cultures—lived on this land. The many communities of Aboriginal peoples had different ways of living, in the different environments they occupied. The Haida of the West Coast fished and hunted for sea mammals, while the First Nations living on the plains hunted for buffalo. In the areas now known as Ontario and Quebec, some First Nations peoples built longhouses and combined agriculture and hunting.

The different nations had their own values, spirituality and traditions, and methods of passing their traditional knowledge and values among families and clans. Today, many Aboriginal peoples living in Canada work to maintain their languages, cultures, values, and traditions in a changing Canada.

Let's Discuss

Many First Nations peoples live on one of over 2200 reserves. Name the First Nations communities that are located near you.

◀ First Nations participate in a powwow at Wikwemikong reserve on Manitoulin Island.

status Indians: People who are registered under the *Indian Act* as members of a particular First Nation; they have the right to live on a specific Indian reserve but may choose to live off the reserve and still retain status.

First Nations: Distinct nations of people sharing common ancestry such as Mi'kmaq, Dene, Mohawk, Cree, Ojibway, Siksika (Blackfoot); replaces the term *Indian*.

Inuit: Aboriginal people who live in Arctic Canada, Northern Quebec, and Labrador.

Métis: Aboriginal people whose ancestors were of mixed heritage (First Nations or Inuit, and European) and whose culture is distinctly Métis.

assimilation: The absorbing of a minority group into the majority.

Aboriginal Self-Definition

Aboriginal people often define their identities through their different languages and cultures—which include their stories, lands, lakes, rivers, and meeting places—and their spiritual connections. These languages and cultures differ across Canada.

Government "Defining" Aboriginals

Outside of Aboriginal communities, other groups have tried throughout Canada's history to identify Aboriginal people clearly. In 1876, just after Confederation, the Canadian government passed the *Indian Act*. This *Act* placed First Nations (registered Indians) under the control of the federal government. Over the years, Aboriginal people have been defined by treaties, laws, and court decisions, and, since 1982, the *Canadian Charter of Rights and Freedoms*. Three of the major categories of Aboriginal people defined in legislation are **status Indians (First Nations), Inuit,** and **Métis**.

▲ Chiefs from across Canada gather in 2003 to choose the new leader for the Assembly of First Nations (see page 119).

Status Indians

The government of Canada recognizes 610 First Nations bands—such as Mi'kmaq, Iroquois (Haudenosaunee), Ojibway (Anishinnabe), Cree, Sioux, Dene, Siksika (Blackfoot), and Haida—representing over 60 different First Nations living on over 2200 reserves. The registered members of these First Nations are status Indians. Some status Indians have left their home reserves to work in towns and cities. They retain their status even when they live off the reserve. There are some benefits to living on reserves, but reserves are often isolated and far from jobs. Since more jobs are available off the reserve, many people choose to leave. But living off the reserve often leads to **assimilation** of Aboriginal people.

The Inuit

The Inuit are native to Canada's north and have their own language and culture. Inuit communities are located across the northern coasts and islands of Canada—from the Yukon in the west to Labrador in the east, with vast distances of mainly rock, water, and ice separating communities from each other. The new territory of Nunavut was created on April 1, 1999. The Inuit are a majority in this territory, and so they have a strong influence on that government. Nunavut was given large powers of self-government over the territory's education, justice systems, and natural resources.

▲ Paul Okalik, premier of Nunavut, holds a replica of a coin commemorating the birth of Nunavut in 1999.

The Métis

Métis people received recognition by the government of Canada under the *Canadian Charter of Rights and Freedoms* in 1982 and again after the Royal Commission on Aboriginal Peoples in 1996. Métis are the descendants of intermarriage between Europeans and Aboriginals. The term Métis comes from an old French word meaning mixed. Métis people have struggled to be recognized as distinct peoples with inherent rights since the time of the two Riel rebellions in western Canada in 1869 and 1885. In 2003, the Supreme Court of Canada officially recognized the existence of the Métis people with rights under the *Charter*.

▲ The Métis symbol dates back to the early 19th century. The horizontal figure eight is the infinity symbol, suggesting that the Métis people will exist forever.

Some Aboriginal Terms

Over time, other terms have been used to discuss the identities and rights of Aboriginal people in Canada.

Aboriginal peoples are the indigenous inhabitants of Canada. This is an inclusive term that is used when referring to First Nations, Inuit, and Métis, so we need to be careful when using this inclusive term.

First Nations replaces the term "Indians." First Nations people can be status, treaty, or non-status. They are distinct nations of people sharing common Native ancestry such as Mi'kmaq, Dene, Mohawk, Cree, Ojibway, Siksika (Blackfoot). But First Nations does not include the Inuit or Métis.

Non-status Indians are not registered as Indians under the *Indian Act*. Their ancestors gave up their Indian status to be able to vote and were removed from a list of status Indians, or they were not originally registered after treaties were signed with the government of Canada.

Treaty Indians are First Nations people whose ancestors signed treaties with the British or Canadian government, either before or after Confederation in 1867.

Non-treaty Indians are First Nations people whose ancestors did not sign treaties with the British or Canadian government. Large parts of British Columbia are non-treaty regions.

◀ This dancer is in traditional First Nations regalia.

Aboriginal Communities Across Canada

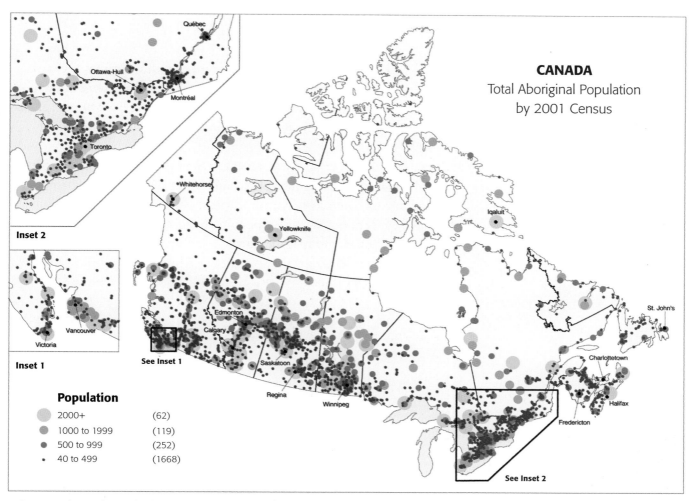

CANADA
Total Aboriginal Population
by 2001 Census

Inset 2

Inset 1

Population

	2000+	(62)
	1000 to 1999	(119)
	500 to 999	(252)
	40 to 499	(1668)

See Inset 1

See Inset 2

The map above shows the location of Aboriginal communities across Canada. The table below shows the numbers of Inuit, Métis, and First Nations in Canada in 2001.

Aboriginal People in Canada, 2001	
Inuit	45 070
Métis	292 310
First Nations	608 850
Total	**946 230**

How Are Aboriginal Peoples' Rights Determined in Canada?

While status Indians have specific rights to live on reserves granted under the *Indian Act*, Inuit and Métis people do not have this special status. They share the same rights as all Canadian citizens, but under the *Canadian Charter of Rights and Freedoms*, they may claim special rights to support their way of life.

These rights include fewer hunting, fishing, and trapping restrictions, Inuktitut (the language of the Inuit) broadcasting, and educational support for Aboriginal people living in the far north. They have often been gained through court challenges. National organizations, such as the Inuit Tapiriit Kanatami and the Métis Council of Canada, work on behalf of their members. The federal government funds many Aboriginal organizations that provide many worthwhile programs to support Aboriginal peoples' needs in communities.

ᐃᓄᐃᑦ ᑕᐱᕇᑦ ᑲᓇᑕᒥ
INUIT TAPIRIIT KANATAMI

▲ This is the logo of the Inuit Tapiriit Kanatami, the national organization of the Inuit. It shows four Inuit surrounding a white maple leaf. The logo was created in 2002 following a contest held across the Arctic.

Aboriginal Communities

Aboriginal communities face many of the same challenges as other rural and urban centres:

- Do they have adequate access to clean water?
- Are roads safe?
- Are schools adequate?
- Is health care available?
- Are housing needs being met?
- Are social services in place?
- Does the community have recreation facilities and a community hall for meetings?
- Can the community raise enough money for new programs?
- Do cultural programs exist?
- Is language instruction available?

Let's Discuss

Choose one First Nations reserve and research how these questions are answered. Share your findings with the class.

▲ Inuit gather for a council meeting at Cape Dorset in Nunavut.

On the reserves, elected band councils make decisions for the community. These band councils have recently been given more power over the way their communities work. The money to make the councils' decisions work comes from the federal government. Other funds come from provincial gambling casinos, such as Casino Rama on the Rama Reserve near Orillia, Ontario. Short-term grants sustain many worthwhile community-run programs, such as preschools, programs for the elderly, adult training and education, and healing centres.

Isolated communities often have different concerns from those of communities located closer to urban centres:

- The reserve may be accessible only by a single road, by air, or by water.

- Hospitals may be hundreds of kilometres away.

- Secondary schooling is often only available off the reserve.

- Jobs may be seasonal, if available at all.

- Training for specific skills and services is lacking.

- There can be problems linked with poverty and isolation, such as illness, alcohol abuse, violence, and suicide.

In facing these problems, many communities have developed new cultural programs employing traditional healing practices over the past decade. Despite the help these services can provide to specific individuals, many communities require both government support and community leadership and skills.

▲ Many Aboriginal communities are isolated, such as this Inuit community of Arctic Bay on Baffin Island in Nunavut.

Rituals of Renewal: Aboriginal Head Start Programs for Preschoolers

Peter Matoush adjusts his green basketball jersey before solemnly picking up a bowl filled with burning sage. As the 5-year-old goes around the circle, his classmates draw the sacred smoke to their faces and over their heads with tiny hands.

Learning the language and cultural teachings of their Ojibway ancestors, these preschool children at the Wabnong site of the Aboriginal Head Start program in Toronto are part of a national initiative aimed at reversing generations of alienation.

For decades, the Canadian government outlawed First Nations languages and ceremonies. Children were sent to residential schools or placed in white foster homes to speed assimilation.

Racism, poverty, and loss of identity have had serious consequences for the Aboriginal population. The results include higher rates of suicide, substance abuse, homelessness, trouble with the law, high-school dropouts, and health problems than Canadians in general.

"There's not a lot of Aboriginal good news stories, but this is definitely one," says Richard Budgell, Health Canada's national manager of the Aboriginal Head Start program for urban and northern communities. The 98 sites across the country where the program is in place are already showing signs of success, he says.

Questions

1. Why are elements of Aboriginal culture introduced to kindergarten-aged Ojibway children in Toronto?

2. Why do you think it can be so difficult to retain Aboriginal culture in cities?

3. What other Aboriginal social issues do Canadians need to address?

◄ Children participate in the Head Start program in Toronto (Wabnong), with JoAnn Kakekayash, an elder in the program.

The White Paper

In 1968, Pierre Trudeau became prime minister. He and his minister of Indian Affairs, Jean Chrétien, were determined to improve the lives of the Aboriginal population of Canada. They believed that discrimination against Aboriginal people was partly to blame for poor economic and social conditions. They felt that discrimination would be reduced if First Nations gave up their registered status and received the same rights as other Canadian citizens. Reserves would be eliminated, and First Nations people would become part of mainstream Canadian society.

In 1969, the government prepared a draft document of proposed changes to laws, called a White Paper. It suggested that the government do away with, or repeal, the *Indian Act*. Some of its suggestions included ideas about inequality, poverty, and citizenship.

Inequality

The separate legal status of First Nations has kept them separated from other Canadians. They have not had the benefits of full citizens of the communities in which they live.

Poverty

Different status for First Nations has resulted in poverty and frustration.

Timeline: Aboriginal Issues

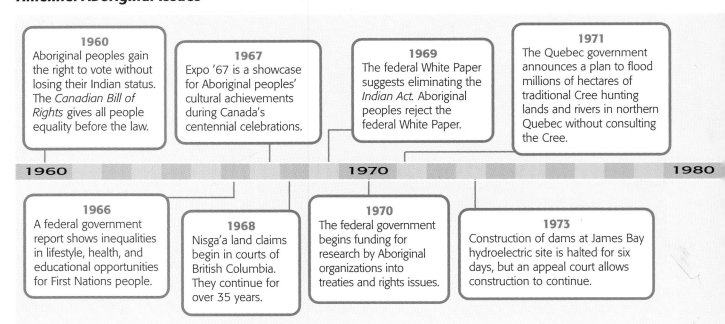

1960
Aboriginal peoples gain the right to vote without losing their Indian status. The *Canadian Bill of Rights* gives all people equality before the law.

1967
Expo '67 is a showcase for Aboriginal peoples' cultural achievements during Canada's centennial celebrations.

1969
The federal White Paper suggests eliminating the *Indian Act*. Aboriginal peoples reject the federal White Paper.

1971
The Quebec government announces a plan to flood millions of hectares of traditional Cree hunting lands and rivers in northern Quebec without consulting the Cree.

1960   1970   1980

1966
A federal government report shows inequalities in lifestyle, health, and educational opportunities for First Nations people.

1968
Nisga'a land claims begin in courts of British Columbia. They continue for over 35 years.

1970
The federal government begins funding for research by Aboriginal organizations into treaties and rights issues.

1973
Construction of dams at James Bay hydroelectric site is halted for six days, but an appeal court allows construction to continue.

Citizenship

The government will offer another road for First Nations people—that of full Canadian citizenship, with all its rights and privileges.

Rejection of the White Paper

Aboriginal leaders universally rejected the report. They claimed that eliminating their legal status as Indians would indeed lead to their assimilation into mainstream Canadian society, but this would mean the loss of their own culture. Loss of their reserves would mean the loss of their connection to the land—the basis for many First Nations people's sense of identity and, eventually, for self-determination. In the face of so much opposition, the government withdrew the White Paper.

First Nations associations, such as the Assembly of First Nations, became much more active in public affairs after the release of the White Paper. Cree author Harold Cardinal's book, *The Unjust Society,* was published that same year. It criticized the federal government and the White Paper. The Assembly of First Nations continues to research treaties and helps lawyers involved in cases affecting Aboriginal rights and land claims. It also helps fund friendship and cultural centres, and works with provincial organizations and band chiefs.

▲ Harold Cardinal attends a First Nations meeting in 1975 in Calgary.

Literacy Strategy

Use the timeline to help you identify the main ideas. Jot these down on a graphic organizer of your choice, and provide supporting details. Use your notes to help you review the topic when you have finished the unit.

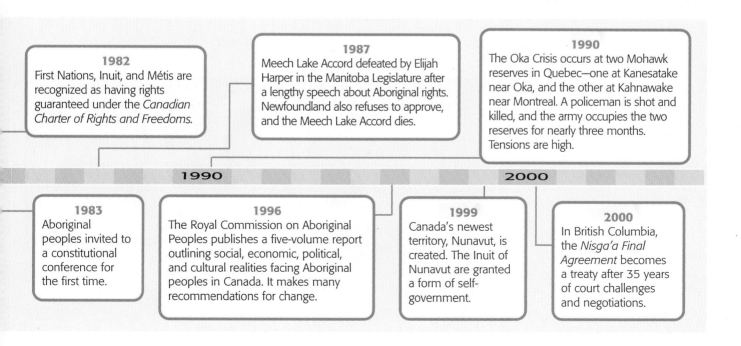

1982
First Nations, Inuit, and Métis are recognized as having rights guaranteed under the *Canadian Charter of Rights and Freedoms.*

1987
Meech Lake Accord defeated by Elijah Harper in the Manitoba Legislature after a lengthy speech about Aboriginal rights. Newfoundland also refuses to approve, and the Meech Lake Accord dies.

1990
The Oka Crisis occurs at two Mohawk reserves in Quebec—one at Kanesatake near Oka, and the other at Kahnawake near Montreal. A policeman is shot and killed, and the army occupies the two reserves for nearly three months. Tensions are high.

1990   2000

1983
Aboriginal peoples invited to a constitutional conference for the first time.

1996
The Royal Commission on Aboriginal Peoples publishes a five-volume report outlining social, economic, political, and cultural realities facing Aboriginal peoples in Canada. It makes many recommendations for change.

1999
Canada's newest territory, Nunavut, is created. The Inuit of Nunavut are granted a form of self-government.

2000
In British Columbia, the *Nisga'a Final Agreement* becomes a treaty after 35 years of court challenges and negotiations.

Aboriginal Self-Government

Since 1960, the relationship between Canada's Aboriginal peoples and the rest of the country has seen many changes. Aboriginal leaders and the Canadian government continue to try to find better ways to deal with a variety of issues. No single solution fits every community. Different Aboriginal groups had different structures for governing. But they did have some things in common. Some distinctive features of these structures include

autonomy: personal independence or freedom

- individual **autonomy** and responsibility
- the rule of law
- the role of women
- the prominent role of elders
- the role of family and clan
- leadership
- the role of consensus in decision making
- the maintenance of traditional institutions

Imposed Actions

In the past, Canadian governments and citizens assumed that our laws and policies would "improve" the lives of Aboriginal peoples. This was often wrong. Governments and business made mistakes when they put the rights of the majority ahead of those of the Aboriginal peoples. The *Canadian Charter of Rights and Freedoms* now guarantees Aboriginal rights, even in cases when these appear to go "against" the rights of the majority.

▶ Ellen Gabriel (centre) was the spokesperson for the Mohawk First Nation in its standoff against the government during the 1990 Oka Crisis. This was a dispute over traditional Mohawk lands.

Aboriginal Community Concerns

Across Canada, Aboriginal communities and leaders face complex issues and try to address concerns that touch on many areas, including

- the environment
- culture
- land claims
- health issues
- education
- hunting and fishing rights
- child care
- support for families and individuals
- employment opportunities

Aboriginal leadership is stronger today than it has been in the past century. Politicians, business leaders, churches, and educators realize we must acknowledge and understand the cultural differences between Aboriginal and non-Aboriginal peoples. Students must learn in schools and from the media about the important issues that affect Aboriginal peoples in their community or region and in Canada as a whole.

Literacy Strategy

After reading, think about what you have read. Take time to reflect on the content, and summarize your thoughts. Can you think of ways to make connections between the topic and the world around you?

▲ Aboriginal teens are studying at a school in their community. Education is one of the main concerns of Aboriginal communities and leaders.

Civics Now DVD

"Healing Justice" from *Civics Now DVD*.

The Federal Government Position

Aboriginal people see their bands as nations, and many feel that the bands should govern themselves. The federal government does not agree. It believes that since it created the elected band council structure, the band councils' powers and authority come from the federal government.

First Nations governments operate much like municipal governments. In fact, they generally act as agents of the federal government. The federal government sees First Nations governments as existing mainly to deliver services to the members of the band. There is much debate about whether the federal government should expand the powers of those governments. Currently, they have fairly wide-ranging powers, and these continue to grow. The *Canadian Charter of Rights and Freedoms* recognizes Aboriginal governments as a third level of government, after federal and provincial.

The Citizenship Issue

The question "Who is an 'Indian'?" is not as simple as it seems. In the legal sense, under the *Indian Act*, some people have not been recognized in the past.

- First Nations people who got the right to vote before 1960 lost Indian status.

- First Nations women who married men who did not have Indian status prior to 1985 lost their status.

- First Nations children lost their status because they were born to an unwed mother or were adopted by a non-Aboriginal family.

- First Nations people who were left off band lists or for some reason were not registered as Indians lost their status.

All these people lost out on some of the benefits of being registered as status Indians. Status Indians can vote in band elections and share in any revenues that the reserve might produce. In addition, it is culturally important for a First Nations person to maintain his or her identity as a status Indian.

▲ Elected Chief Lorraine McRae of the Chippewas of Mnjikaning is seen here with a veteran at a ceremony at the Rama Reserve.

Citizenship: Who Decides?

First Nations leaders want the power to decide who is an "Indian". Aboriginal identity means certain rights and responsibilities. That is why the identity issue is really about citizenship. A status Indian is a citizen governed under the terms of the *Indian Act*. Citizens form independent governments that have authority and are equal to other governments. The aim of First Nations people is self-government.

A fundamental point in the disputes between Aboriginal peoples and the Canadian government is that Aboriginal peoples claim that they have the right to determine who can become a citizen of their community. The Canadian government claims that it alone has that right and is the only sovereign government of the country. Who is right?

The *Canadian Charter of Rights and Freedoms* guarantees equal rights and freedoms to all Canadians, including Aboriginal peoples. Beyond that, the *Charter* also recognizes and guarantees Aboriginal and treaty rights, such as land claims agreements.

Partition of Quebec

Another aspect of Aboriginal citizenship appeared in the late 1990s. When Quebec separatist leaders were talking about leaving Canada and setting up their own state, the Cree of Northern Quebec had a shock for them. They said that if Canada were divisible, then so was Quebec, and they would stay with Canada. Cree Chief Matthew Coon Come stated that the Quebec government could not claim traditional Cree lands and could not declare the Cree to be citizens of a separate Quebec.

Let's Discuss

Who should have the right to decide who can be a member or citizen of a particular group?

◄ First Nations leaders Matthew Coon Come (right) and Elijah Harper discuss a variety of issues at an annual Assembly of First Nations meeting.

Elijah Harper

In 1990, a citizen not widely known outside of his province rocketed to national fame. He was a First Nation Manitoban named Elijah Harper. The Meech Lake Accord had to be passed by all ten provinces by June 23, 1990, to become law. Harper was the lone Aboriginal member of the Legislative Assembly of Manitoba. He opposed the Accord because he believed that it did not recognize the distinct status of Aboriginal people the way it recognized that of Quebec.

Harper blocked the passage of the Accord by refusing to vote for it before the June deadline. Since the Accord needed the approval of all provinces, Harper's action effectively defeated it. This put Aboriginal peoples' concern—and their desire to be Canadian citizens, but of a different kind and with different rights—alongside Quebec's on Canada's centre stage.

Questions

1. How did Elijah Harper promote the interests of a minority over the will of the majority?

2. In a democracy, is it fair that one person can deny the will of the majority? Why or why not?

▲ Elijah Harper holds an eagle feather, symbolizing spiritual strength, during the Meech Lake debate in the Manitoba legislature, in June 1990.

Self-Government After Meech Lake

Elijah Harper's opposition to the Meech Lake Accord defeated it. But Prime Minister Brian Mulroney tried once more to revise the Constitution. This time, Aboriginal self-government was included in the agreement called the Charlottetown Accord. It did not define what self-government meant. In any case, this Accord was defeated in a national referendum in 1992.

Apology from the Government

Since then, Aboriginal peoples have made some gains in their goal of self-government. In 1996, the Royal Commission on Aboriginal Peoples helped make the public aware of many issues. Two years later, the federal government issued a Statement of Reconciliation, apologizing for past mistakes, such as the attempts to assimilate Aboriginal people.

▲ In January 1998, federal Indian Affairs Minister Jane Stewart publicly apologized to Aboriginal people for past government actions. With her is Phil Fontaine, grand chief of the Assembly of First Nations.

Aboriginal Claims

In 1998, after 30 years of negotiations, the Nisga'a signed a treaty with British Columbia and the federal government. The treaty was officially **ratified** by Parliament in 2000. In this treaty, the Nisga'a were given wide powers of self-government in matters of culture, language, and family life.

Many Aboriginal land claims in the North have been settled, and others are before the courts. Each of these agreements includes some elements of Aboriginal self-government. This Aboriginal goal of attaining the "inherent right to self-government" does not mean that Aboriginal peoples want independence from Canada, but, rather, a right to govern themselves within Canada.

Louis Stevenson, Chief of the Pequis Band of Manitoba, denied that First Nations wanted outright independence. He acknowledged the roles of the federal and provincial governments. But he also pointed out that First Nations have control of certain matters on their reserves. Where powers overlap, the various governments will share responsibilities.

ratified: to approve or confirm formally

▲ Louis Stevenson was the Chief of the Pequis Band in Manitoba.

⟷ Check Your Understanding

1. Read the material on the 1969 White Paper on pages 118–119.

   a) How does the White Paper show that the federal government was well intentioned?

   b) Why do you think that First Nations leaders opposed the terms of the paper so strenuously?

2. Canadian governmental functions are currently shared among three governments: the federal, provincial, and municipal (see Unit 2, "The Informed Citizen," for a discussion of the levels of government). Which functions do you think Aboriginal peoples would want their own governments to control in order to help solve their economic, cultural, and social problems? Which functions do you think the provincial and federal governments would want to keep? Why?

3. Do you think it was important for the Canadian government to issue an apology to the Aboriginal peoples for past mistakes? Explain your answer.

Ecohabits

Lumbering Native Lands

Some First Nations groups have been able to resist outsiders entering the lands they have been granted by treaty. When the group has no legal standing under the *Indian Act*, however, problems can arise. That is what happened to the 500-member Lubicon Cree, non-status Indians who live in Northern Alberta.

The Lubicon have never signed a treaty surrendering their traditional lands. In 1986, the Alberta government leased huge tracts of land, including 10 000 square kilometres of traditional Lubicon hunting and trapping territories to 12 forestry companies. Clear-cutting logging practices will devastate the traditional hunting and trapping practices that sustain the Lubicon Cree.

- In 1988, Friends of the Lubicon was organized to challenge regulatory practices and logging methods of a large multinational company.

- In 1991, the Friends began a boycott campaign against paper bags manufactured by the multinational company.

- The boycott lasted for four years, resulting in over $5 million in lost sales.

- The Friends work in conjunction with the Lubicon leadership to delay clear-cut logging.

Protesters support the Lubicon Cree in their fight against the Alberta government for allowing logging companies to clear-cut on their traditional lands.

Questions

1. Suggest several tactics the Lubicon could use (e.g., media publicity campaign, petitions, or letter of protest to the government) to get justice. Discuss how each of these methods could help the Lubicon cause. Defend your answers with examples.

2. Write a letter that could be sent to a newspaper. In it, outline the problems the Lubicon are facing. Share the letter with your class.

Skills *for* Social *Action*

Values Exploration

When studying civic issues, you must consider many different viewpoints. You also have to explore the values on which these viewpoints are based. Values are qualities or characteristics that you consider crucial to your identity and your life.

Your Personal Values

Look at your own values and those of your entire community or nation. Some examples of your own personal values may be

- realization of your own worth
- curiosity
- concern for personal health
- open-mindedness
- love of beauty (art, music, literature)
- sense of identity

- hope in the future
- love of learning
- desire for financial gain
- independent thinking
- pride in your family, ethnic, cultural, and/or national background

Social Values

Some examples of social values may be

- peace
- tolerance
- national identity
- environmental consciousness
- commitment to personal and political freedoms

- justice for all
- respect for privacy
- economic opportunity
- respect for the law
- respect for the dignity and worth of all people

Exploring the personal and social values underlying an issue will help you to understand why your viewpoint may differ from someone else's. It will also help to clarify why societies act in a certain way in dealing with civic conflict.

Steps You Can Take

Step 1: With the help of your teacher, choose a provocative statement, a problem, or an issue described in the text (e.g., in a "Speaking Out" or a "Civics Showcase") or choose any civic issue of interest to you (e.g., laws that ban teens from smoking).

Step 2: Identify and clarify the issue. Explain how this is a civic issue and not just a personal one. For example, many people in society want to stop teens from smoking because of the health risks. It is legal to purchase cigarettes in Canada at age 19. The government makes a lot of money from high taxes on cigarettes. The health care system pays for the future health effects of smoking.

Step 3: Describe the multiple viewpoints on the issue. For example, teens should be able to choose for themselves. Teens are not old enough to make a decision that will affect their future health so the government must protect them from their own bad choices.

Step 4: What is your viewpoint? Explain why this is your viewpoint. Identify the personal values that affect your view.

Step 5: Consider possible choices for civic action regarding this issue (e.g., increase penalties for selling cigarettes to minors, fine teens caught smoking, make it difficult to smoke outside of your own home, raise the price of cigarettes, create an anti-smoking campaign aimed at teens, fine parents who let their children smoke, give a cash bonus to those teens who quit smoking, provide free quit-smoking kits and support in high schools).

Step 6: Discuss how each choice might affect you, your society, and the world.

Step 7: Which choice(s) for civic action would you support?

Step 8: What values underlie your choice? What values might underlie each of the other choices (e.g., personal choice/freedom, healthy living, respect for the law, or respect for others)?

Step 9: Why did you make the choice you did? Be sure to consider your own opinions, such as political, religious and cultural beliefs, personal goals, life experiences, and the influence of others in your life.

Step 10: Present and defend your choice(s).

Skills for Social *Action*

Conducting an Interview

An interview is often the best way to get information about an issue. A local politician, a school administrator, or a community leader can often tell you things that printed sources cannot match. Good interviews depend on thorough preparation and effective questioning. Let's consider the steps to get ready for an interview.

Suppose you are investigating a development project in your community. A large developer has proposed to build a new subdivision, and citizens have differing opinions about it. You have arranged an interview with a local councillor to discuss the issue. Make sure you tell the councillor how you will be using the interview.

Preparation

1. Find information about the topic before the interview. Read reports and the letters to the editor in your local newspaper. Check Web sites, blogs, and the like. Talk with other people about the issue. For example, you might find out that some citizens think that the subdivision will bring in more taxes and allow the community to provide more services. Others may oppose the increased traffic it will bring to town or the loss of green space.

2. Prepare several key questions for your interview based on your preliminary research:

   • Why was this area considered for the subdivision?

   • How much money will this produce in extra taxes?

   • What plans are in place for increased traffic flow?

   Be prepared to follow up on these key questions with others as the interview proceeds. For example, if the interviewee replies that the project will produce a certain amount in new taxes, ask how local council plans to spend that money.

3. Arrange a convenient time and place for the interview. Make it clear to the person what information you want, especially if the issue is a controversial one. You might even tell the person the key questions you will be asking before the interview.

The Interview

4. Recording the interview can help you to make sure you remember what the person said. Ask whether you can use an audio or video recorder before the interview. Some people are comfortable with them, while others are not. Respect the feelings of the interviewee on this matter.

5. Dress appropriately, and arrive on time for the interview. Set a time limit for the interview, and stay within it. Remember that the person you are interviewing is busy, but may be too polite to say so.

6. Listen carefully to the person, occasionally asking follow-up questions to the answers. Be more than just a recorder of his or her opinions and ideas.

7. As soon as possible after the interview, develop your notes into a report, while it is still fresh in your mind. Do not forget to send a thank-you note to the person you interviewed. It would also be courteous to send him or her a copy of your report.

Unit Conclusion

1. When asking citizens' opinions on an issue, governments may ask the question in a way that makes it easier for them to get the answer they want. Suppose you wanted to hold a referendum in your school about, say, school uniforms. How would you word the question to get people to give the answer you want?

2. List five reasons federalism and being part of Canada is good for young Quebec francophones. List five ways it is not.

3. Here are the main provisions of the 1992 referendum. Read through them carefully. Decide whether you would vote for or against the Charlottetown Accord of 1992 and give your reasons.

   • Quebec would be recognized as a distinct society.

   • Aboriginal peoples would be given the right to negotiate self-government.

   • The Senate would be elected, not appointed; provinces would be given equal representation in Parliament.

   • Aboriginal peoples would be given special representation within the Senate.

   • Any Senate bills affecting French language or culture would be subject to francophone veto.

   • Quebec would be guaranteed 25 percent of the seats in the House of Commons.

4. Do interest groups help or hinder the efforts of citizens who want change? Defend your position with real examples if possible.

5. Surveys of public opinion indicate that most Quebeckers identify first with their province, and then with Canada. Many non-Quebeckers identify first with Canada, and then with their province. Does this difference weaken Canada? Explain.

6. Investigate the history of the reserve system in Canada. Write a report in which you support or oppose it, giving your reasons.

7. Watch the video "The Great Divide" from the *Civics Now DVD,* and then answer the following questions:

a) Research the positions on the partition of Quebec held by

   i)   English Quebeckers

   ii) Aboriginal Quebeckers

   iii) French Quebeckers

   iv) a federal government representative

b) Explain how groups i and ii see their citizenship being affected if Quebec separates and does not partition.

c) If you were a non-Quebecker, what position would you take on

   i)   separation of Quebec

   ii) partition of Quebec

d) Consider how your rights as a citizen might be affected by the developments suggested in c).

e) Do you think that it is possible to have different types of Canadian citizenship? For example, could there be one for Aboriginal peoples, another for minorities such as English Quebeckers, and another for French Quebeckers? Or must one model fit all Canadians? Discuss.

The Global Citizen

Focus Questions

This unit explores these questions:

- *How can the globe be a village?*

- *Do the media help or hinder our understanding of world issues?*

- *What are some of the critical issues facing our world?*

- *How can you stand up for human rights?*

- *How are conflict resolution and peace linked?*

- *What is an environmental citizen?*

- *What challenges face the world's indigenous people?*

- *When are certain forms of political protest warranted and useful?*

- *How does the UN promote the rights and responsibilities of global citizenship?*

- *What is Canada's role in the global community?*

What Is This Unit About?

Do you think a peaceful world is possible? Do you think people can treat one another and the environment with respect? Will you reach adulthood in a world where all nations and people tackle global issues head-on and cooperatively? Or will selfish and thoughtless people ignore crucial global problems?

People around the world are more closely connected now than they have ever been. Travel, immigration, and improved communications, such as the Internet, allow us to see global challenges firsthand. Defining and fulfilling global needs is challenging. Complex issues must be considered in making any decisions. Not becoming involved may result in the loss of entire societies or the planet itself. A good global citizen becomes actively involved in world issues. How will you get involved?

Key Terms

annexed	inequitable	peacekeeping
arbitrary	interconnected	petition
diversity	interdependent	reenfranchised
genocide	multinational corporations	sustainability
Holocaust	non-government organization (NGO)	vigil
human rights		

4.1 | You as a Global Citizen

Focus Question

- *How can the globe be a village?*

The Global Village

You may have heard the world referred to as the "global village." Canadian thinker Marshall McLuhan invented this term back in the 1960s. But what does it mean? A village is a small group of people who share a common set of values that helps them to survive and develop. But the globe is a vast place, filled with many different kinds of people and groups. So, how can it be a village?

Interrelated World

The global village is a simple concept. We are all part of an **interconnected** and **interdependent** community, in every part of the globe. We can find out the scores of European soccer matches in the middle of the night, and we can hear yesterday's music concert from Bangkok on our MP3 player today. Everything, from what we wear, to what we eat, to the friends we have at school, reflects how the parts of the world are interrelated.

To improve our world community, all parts of the globe need to cooperate. We have a responsibility as citizens of a global village. We must work to develop a world with justice and peace for all. By focusing on our common needs, we can begin to break down barriers between ourselves and others.

▲ Our global village is an interconnected community.

Education to Action: The Global Citizen

The first important step in global citizenship is to try to understand the questions facing the world. But where do we start? We have to educate ourselves about the problems that we face together. The survival of our global village depends on many key factors:

- economic justice
- health
- **peacekeeping** and conflict resolution
- human rights
- ecological balance
- social and political movements

These issues are as interdependent and interconnected as are the people of the world—the global village we have been discussing. For example, the problem of hunger affects many other things. If a group of people cannot get enough food, they may decide to leave their homes in search of it. That could lead to disorder and confusion. Local services often cannot cope with the changes.

More than Education

It is important to remember that education by itself cannot improve our world. Changing things takes coordinated action on the part of global citizens. You can respond personally in any number of ways:

- Join an organization that represents a cause important to you.
- Take part in events to promote that cause.
- Write letters to people in power.

Local Changes

You can work at the community level and make changes in your life that will have an effect on society and the world. Small efforts can help change the world. These could be actions such as recycling your pop cans or standing up against racism in your school and community. It is up to you to decide how deeply you want to be involved in global issues that may at first appear complex and overwhelming.

We often hear the phrase, "think globally, act locally." What does this mean? It means just what we were discussing about the global village and our interconnected world. Global problems are often too overwhelming (and far away) for us to make sense of. But sometimes we can do small things in our community (locally) that will change things elsewhere (globally).

---

peacekeeping: The overseeing of a halt in fighting between nations or groups; Canadian Lester Pearson won the Nobel Peace Prize for "inventing" modern peacekeeping.

Let's Discuss

There has always been (and probably always will be) conflict between different groups in society. Everyone's actions affect how things turn out. If you do not get involved, you are not neutral—you are siding with the powerful. Think of an event in your life involving people with a lot of power and people with a little power. What side were you on? Did anyone try to remain neutral? What effect did this have? Report your experience to your class.

Civics Now DVD

"Algeria"
from *Civics Now DVD.*

Educating the Global Citizen

"Education for Development promotes the growth of positive attitudes and values in children and young people. It also gives them the knowledge and skills that will let them promote these values. This will bring about change in their own lives and in their communities, both locally and globally."

"Children's education should include the development of respect for human rights and freedoms. It should also develop respect for other cultures and for the natural environment."

Questions

1. To what extent does your high school experience reflect these statements?
2. What courses have you taken that have helped you develop global awareness and caring?
3. What other courses might you take in the future to develop your global awareness?

▲ Students learn respect for human rights, freedom, other cultures, and the environment.

Views of the World

These maps provide different ways to look at our world. What viewpoints do these maps show? What information do the maps provide? What world issues do these maps illustrate? Make a prediction based on one of the maps.

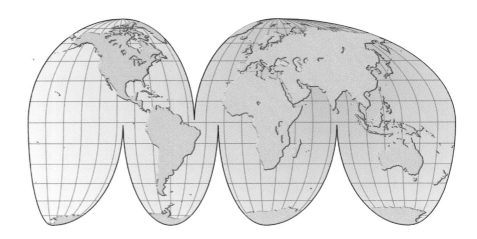

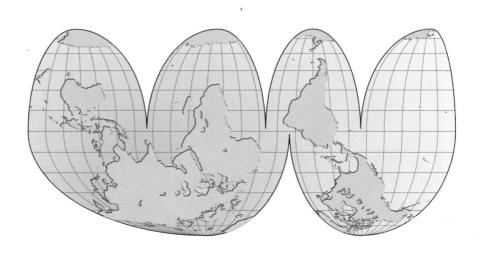

Let's Discuss

United Nations statistics suggest that about a billion people are illiterate (a fifth of the world's population). Providing education for all would cost only an additional $7 billion a year—about what is spent in a month by the United States for the war in Iraq. Name one thing you might expect to change if everyone in the world could read and write. Be prepared to defend your answer.

↔ Check Your Understanding

1. Explain in your own words the phrase "think globally, act locally."
2. List three ways education can make us better global citizens.

4.2 | How the Media Inform Us

Focus Question

- *Do the media help or hinder our understanding of world issues?*

Literacy Strategy

Before reading, jot down your opinions in a chart to help you think about your answer to the Focus Question. After reading, update your chart with more ideas. Think about how you would justify your opinions.

Global Information

Becoming a global citizen involves a serious study of the problems and challenges facing our world. We are used to seeing pictures of starving babies, poverty-stricken communities, and bloody conflicts. These pictures and news reports seem to make us more aware of certain events around the globe. But do they really? Do they provide enough information for us to examine critically the causes of the events? Do they present possible solutions to the problems? Too often, the answer is no.

One-Sided Views

Often, the media present one-sided views of the people in other countries. After we are flooded with images of disasters and misfortunes around the world, we might begin to think of our global neighbours as helpless victims. We might begin to wonder why they are unable to solve their own problems. Why are they in constant need of assistance from us? In reality, people in all nations, rich or poor, are engaged in growth and struggle. We are all trying to achieve better lives through community cooperation.

▲ The media flood us with many global stories, but do we always get the full picture?

Distorted News

Media coverage of global issues presents a distorted view. Too often, we get the message that poverty, hunger, or homelessness exist only in other countries. In fact, they also occur in our own neighbourhoods. By focusing on the differences between people instead of on the similarities, we often overlook our shared world concerns. Detailed, fair media coverage must consider several points of view. That way, it will show the similarities (and differences) of people everywhere.

Getting Informed Globally

The media play an essential role in giving us information from around the globe. Fifty years ago, there was little television news coverage. Then, the details of natural disasters such as Hurricane Katrina (2005), or acts of terrorism such as the destruction of the World Trade Center in 2001, would have taken much longer to report.

Disasters such as Hurricane Katrina (above) and the destruction of the World Trade Center (below) were reported immediately worldwide by the media.

Media Diversity

Canada is a nation of immigrants, and its multicultural population demands news from around the world. Many Canadians have connections to family, friends, and organizations in other countries. These contacts also provide viewpoints that differ from those presented in the local Canadian media. This has resulted in Canadian community-based newspapers and television programs, which have a greater number of points of view.

The Internet

The Internet is also a source of information and different viewpoints on global issues. Independent Internet sites offer new and different coverage of events. Most "indy" media sites promote open exchange of information and accept articles from anyone, regardless of the author's skill level and experience in publishing. Weblogs (blogs) and message boards hosted by individuals or groups provide another rich source of information offering different points of view. These often encourage discussion on topics that are sometimes overlooked by mainstream media. But we must always be aware of who is making the statements and claims. How reliable is any source? (For more information on evaluating sources such as the Internet, see pages 20 and 219–220.)

Speaking Out!

The Media's Influence

"The media, especially television, is only out to shock its audience. Fire, floods, famine, wars are great for ratings! People are fascinated by this stuff. People don't really know anything more about the world by watching the news. They just feel grateful not to live in these troubled places. Sure, you might feel guilty enough to send money to some charity, but then you turn off the TV and forget about it. What do we really know about these people and places? There's no thoughtful consideration of the issues as far as I can see."

"The news today is a great source of information on issues of global concern. Whether discussing global warming, the latest peace treaty, or the struggles of a political activist, many newspapers invest considerable time and effort to keep Canadians aware of what's going on with their 'global neighbours.' Specific global problems have been solved, political prisoners freed, famine victims assisted, and governments pressured into change as a result of increased world pressure caused by public awareness through excellent media coverage."

Questions

1. Which speaker do you agree with most? Why?
2. Where do you get your information on global events?
3. Which news sources do you find the most reliable and why?

◀ Some media like to shock us with attention-grabbing reports, but how reliable are they?

↔ Check Your Understanding

1. List two ways the media present one-sided views of people around the world. Research your answers on the Internet and compare with the class.
2. What is the difference between mainstream news sites on the Web and independent news sites on the Web?
3. How has multiculturalism in Canada affected our media? Research local multicultural newspapers to help you answer the question.

Web Links

Information on Media
To learn more about mainstream media, from television networks to print newspapers and independent news Web sites, go to **www.nelson.com/civicsnow.**

4.3 | Contemporary Global Concerns

World Malnutrition

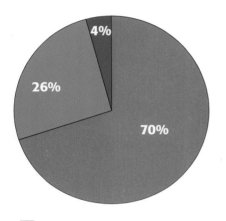

- Asia
- Africa
- Latin America and Caribbean

inequitable: Unequal, unfair.

Focus Question

- *What are some of the critical issues facing our world?*

The world faces a great many critical issues, ranging from violence and warfare to poverty and lack of freedom. Too many of the world's citizens do not have access to food, clothing, and shelter. Others lack education and literacy skills. Inequality can result in hunger, injustice, illness, illiteracy, unemployment, human rights violations, and environmental crises. Of these serious problems, we will concentrate on three: hunger, health, and human rights.

World Hunger

We have more than enough food to feed the entire world's people. But, because of **inequitable** distribution, one in every four of the world's children is malnourished and unhealthy. People in less developed parts of the world often do not have access to the resources to feed themselves and keep themselves healthy. They cannot break out of the cycle of poverty and illness into which they were born.

Hunger and poverty go hand in hand. People go hungry because they have no access to food. They do not have the power to get access to the food they need. They lack the education, fertile land, or technology to feed themselves. It is estimated that about 800 million people around the world are affected by hunger. Malnutrition plays a role in five million child deaths each year.

Local Hunger

Hunger is not limited to developing countries. Right in your community, food banks assist those who cannot afford housing costs, clothes, and food. Hunger will remain a problem until the people of the world get focused on a cooperative effort to eliminate it.

▲ Food banks help many who cannot afford to buy food.

World Health

How can the world cope with the shared problem of disease? The United Nations founded the World Health Organization (WHO) in 1948 to help all people "attain the highest levels of health possible." One of its concerns is the spread of infectious diseases, which know no borders. Against these, prevention is our best defence. The WHO and other organizations have convinced countries to provide vaccines to protect citizens against preventable diseases. World cooperation has saved over 20 million lives in the past two decades.

The Global Outbreak Alert and Response Network, a part of WHO, deals with the spread of epidemics, particularly new diseases. Health care professionals, along with leaders and ordinary citizens of all nations, work together to help prevent diseases. They monitor them and try to find cures for newly identified diseases that affect the global community. For example, in 2005, avian influenza threatened the world. Individuals, organizations, and governments in Asia and North America called for world cooperation to limit the spread of this life-threatening disease.

▲ WHO Director General Lee Jong discusses the avian influenza epidemic of 2005.

World HIV/AIDS Cases, 2004

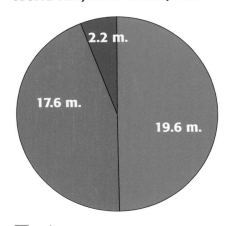

2.2 m.

17.6 m.

19.6 m.

■ Males
■ Females
  Total adult = 37.2 million
■ Children
  Total cases = 30.4 million

Battling HIV/AIDS

One of the greatest challenges in world health today is HIV/AIDS. This virus has infected nearly 40 million people worldwide. The AIDS epidemic has led to fundamental changes in societies everywhere. The United Nations estimated that in 2004, there were nearly five million new infections. More than 95 percent of these were in developing countries.

Of the 3 million HIV/AIDS-related deaths in 2004, over 500 000 were children. The main reason for higher rates of infection in developing countries is lack of education. People living in developing countries also cannot afford the drugs and long-term health care needed to treat the disease.

HIV/AIDS is particularly severe in sub-Saharan Africa, where 6.2 million people between the ages of 15 and 24 live with the disease. Organizations around the world are working with local communities to help stop the spread of AIDS through education about the disease and to alleviate the suffering of those infected and affected.

▲ Students in Uganda learn in class about AIDS.

Making A
Difference

Stephen Lewis

Stephen Lewis is one global citizen who is leading the fight against HIV/AIDS. He is a Canadian who has been a teacher in Africa, leader of the New Democratic Party in Ontario, and a diplomat (Canadian Ambassador to the United Nations). Today, he brings his vast experience and passion about social issues to his job as the UN Secretary General's Special Envoy on HIV/AIDS in Africa.

The Stephen Lewis Foundation works with local African organizations to help bring comfort to those who are sick and dying. It also tries to help orphans and support groups of people living with AIDS. Stephen Lewis's humanitarian efforts include battling the discrimination faced by people with this disease. Part of this involves educating people about the causes and prevention of HIV/AIDS and telling the rest of the world about the plight of these people.

Questions

1. Research the problem of HIV/AIDS, and report back to your class with three ways to prevent the spread of the virus.
2. Name two reasons Stephen Lewis gives for his work in AIDS in Africa. How could you help this important work?

▲ Stephen Lewis is the UN Special Envoy on HIV/AIDS in Africa.

Battling AIDS
To learn more about Stephen Lewis's groundbreaking AIDS work in Africa, go to **www.nelson.com/civicsnow**.

Human Rights

Human rights are defined in several ways, depending on who you ask. But modern democratic societies generally recognize the basic rights and freedoms to which every citizen is entitled. These include such things as life; liberty; freedom of thought, expression, and religion; and equality before the law. This is a complex subject, and many millions of words have been written about it. In general, despite differences of emphasis, it is not too difficult to tell a free society from one that is not free.

Children's Rights

Children have rights, too, although they are not the same as those of adults. But just because minors (people under the age defined by law, such as 18 to vote in Canada) are restricted in certain activities does not mean that they do not have certain basic rights and freedoms. (For more on human rights, read Section 4.4 starting on page 155.)

Child Labour

The UN defines a child as anyone under the age of 18. In many countries in the world, children must work in brutal conditions for the basic necessities. In June 1999, the International Labour Organization (ILO) introduced a program banning the worst forms of child labour, including slavery, prostitution, and forced military recruitment. The treaty urges nations to remove children from harmful work and provide them with basic free education or training.

Human Rights for Children

The International Labour Organization estimates that in developing countries alone, 250 million children between 5 and 14 years old work. About half of these children are believed to work full-time. They work to support themselves and their families. They are too poor to be able to afford to go to school. Therefore, they have little hope of finding better jobs as they mature. Child labour is part of a vicious cycle of poverty.

▲ Young children work in many developing countries around the world.

Web Links

UN *Convention on the Rights of the Child*

To learn more about the UN *Convention on the Rights of the Child,* go to **www.nelson.com/civicsnow**.

Child Slavery

Worldwide, an estimated 100 million children are forced into slavery. Their "owners" demand forced labour to repay small loans. This practice is common throughout parts of Africa and Asia. Children as young as 6 work 16- to 18-hour days, often in dangerous situations. The United Nations reports that 200 000 children are trafficked as slaves annually in West and Central Africa.

"Sex tourism" is the growing commercial exploitation of thousands of children each year by tourists to countries such as Mexico and Thailand. Often, impoverished young girls are forced into unprotected sex. In these nations, the majority of people with AIDS have contracted the virus between the ages of 12 and 18.

▲ Young children work long hours in weaving factories.

Child Poverty

Child poverty affects children in developed countries as well as those in developing countries. Often, even in "wealthy" countries, children and families can be trapped in cycles of poverty. In Australia, Canada, and the United States, over 50 percent of children in a single-parent family headed by a woman are living below the poverty line. In Denmark, Finland, and Sweden, however, where government policies have been developed to address the problem of child poverty, fewer than 10 percent of children live below the poverty line.

▲ Many Canadian teens have jobs, but usually they work out of choice and not out of necessity.

Literacy Strategy

As you read, make connections between the content and the world you live in. Pause and think about the topic and summarize in your own words so you can better understand it.

Web Links

Non-governmental Organizations (NGOs)

To learn more about the many different NGOs operating in various countries around the world, including the courageous members of Médecins Sans Frontières, go to **www.nelson.com/civicsnow**.

Civics Now DVD

"Donation Destination" from *Civics Now DVD*.

▶ A doctor from Médecins Sans Frontières treats a young child in Burundi, in Africa.

Some Solutions

The problems of world hunger, health, and human rights seem overwhelming, but there are some solutions. In the area of child labour, for example, Iqbal Masih and Craig Kielburger have helped publicize the problem and have rescued many children from terrible lives.

Non-governmental Organizations (NGOs)

Some of the organizations that try to make improvements around the world are known as **non-governmental organizations** (NGOs). As the name implies, NGOs are not part of any state government but are generally organized around a common goal. In fact, some refuse to accept any government aid at all; others accept a small amount of state aid. NGOs are self-governing and largely voluntary, with only a small paid staff. Often they are charities, which raise their operating funds through donations from private groups and individuals.

Long-Term Solutions

In any complicated problem, people who help those in need realize that short-term solutions do not provide the answer. Communities want to acquire the tools and knowledge that will enable them to become independent. The dual purpose of voluntary organizations is to provide for those who are hungry, sick, and poor today, as well as to help change the conditions that cause their problems.

Iqbal Masih

When Iqbal Masih was 4 years old, his desperately poor parents sold him into slavery for less than $16. For the next six years, he remained shackled to a carpet-weaving loom, tying tiny knots from 4 A.M. to 6 P.M. Carpet factory owners prefer child workers because their tiny fingers make the smallest, tightest knots and hence the best carpets.

When he was 10, Masih contacted the Bonded Labour Liberation Front, a private group fighting against child labour in Pakistan, and he was able to escape from the factory. By age 12, he was free and travelling the world in his crusade against the horrors of child labour.

But, for freeing thousands of children through his courageous global campaign, Masih received repeated threats from people in the powerful carpet-weaving industry. In 1995, only months after Masih had received worldwide attention and recognition, he was shot dead. His killers were never caught.

Questions

1. Why do you think Iqbal Masih was murdered?
2. Why do you think children are more likely to be abused than adults?

▲ Iqbal Masih became a child's rights advocate at a very young age.

Craig Kielburger

In April 1995, Craig Kielburger read an article about the death of Iqbal Masih on the front page of the *Toronto Star.* Kielburger, who was also 12 years old, was shocked at the cruel life and tragic death of Masih. He looked into the issue of child labour and organized his friends and classmates to form an organization called Free the Children.

Kielburger also arranged a trip to South Asia, which received a lot of media attention. On that trip, he followed social activists who rescued children enslaved in bonded labour, and returned these malnourished and mistreated children to their friends and families. Kielburger founded an effective NGO, educated the people of Canada to the tragedy of child labour, and through his charismatic leadership and commitment, placed this issue into the media spotlight. Free the Children has opened more than 100 schools and rehabilitation centres for freed child labourers.

Questions

1. What do you think is one of the most important qualities of an effective NGO? Why is Free the Children an influential NGO?
2. Find an NGO that you feel is useful, and take action to support its goals.

▲ Craig Kielburger became a champion against child labour after he read about Iqbal Masih's murder.

Think Globally, Act Locally

Traditional sweatshops were factories or workshops that exploited workers with low pay, long hours, and unsafe working conditions. Many such sweatshops continue to take advantage of the desperation that forces workers to accept brutal conditions. Today, "virtual" sweatshops exploit immigrant workers who sew clothing at home, paid by the piece. Most of the workers are female. They make far less than minimum wage and receive no employee benefits.

Groups of socially conscious Canadian students are trying to end sweatshops in Canada and around the world. Student-led groups urge consumers to read labels and find out about a company's treatment of both its workers and the environment before buying its products. Were your running shoes or jeans made in a sweatshop? Many athletic footwear companies and clothing manufacturers have yielded to public pressure regarding unfair labour practices. Governments are also being forced to enforce fair labour laws.

▲ Concerned young people can avoid buying products made in sweatshops by reading labels carefully.

Consumers with Conscience—Buying Fair-Trade Products

You can help end exploitation of workers and bring an end to sweatshops. The next time you have a craving for coffee, chocolate, or a banana, buy a product that is identified as "fair trade." This guarantees that the people working to grow and harvest the product that you consume receive a fair wage and good working conditions. Ensuring that workers receive fair wages will help to eliminate extreme poverty in the world.

An amount from the sales of fair trade goods is paid directly to the workers to provide access to better housing, health care, and education for the communities that work to produce these goods. Fair trade companies also must sign contracts with local communities that allow for long-term planning and production practices that do not harm the environment. Many cosmetic companies also make products whose ingredients (e.g., cocoa butter, shea butter) have been "fair traded." As a consumer with conscience, you can help rather than take advantage of workers in other nations.

▲ Fair-trade centres allow us to buy fair-trade-certified products, such as coffee.

Question
Find three products identified as "fair trade" and tell your class about them. Be sure to explain why they are "fair." Make a list of all the products.

Web Links

Fair Trade
To learn more information about fair trade and fair-traded products, go to
www.nelson.com/civicsnow.

↤ Check Your Understanding

1. What is an NGO?
2. Why do you think some NGOs prefer to remain independent from governments?
3. List three ways in which children and teenagers are victims of economic injustice.
4. In what ways could you help children and workers who are being exploited?

4.4 Human Rights

Focus Question

- *How can you stand up for human rights?*

For basic survival, people need food, clothing, and shelter. But for full and meaningful lives, they also need many other important things. Democratic societies protect and maintain many rights and freedoms. These include freedom of speech; freedom of the press; freedom of religion; freedom of association; and the right to life, liberty, and security of person.

Together, these are known as **human rights.** Other human rights include economic, social, and cultural rights. Some people include the right to leisure and rest and the right to social security, such as employment insurance and health care.

Civics Now DVD

"Hostages"
from *Civics Now DVD.*

▲ These people are protesting for human rights in Pakistan.

Essential Rights

Human rights are essential to our growth as individuals and to the growth of our global community. Respect for human rights and human dignity is the foundation of freedom, justice, and peace.

It is hard for us to believe that there was once a time in Canada when slavery existed, when children worked long hours in factories, or when women, Aboriginal peoples, and other ethnic groups were not allowed to vote. Conditions have changed because citizens put pressure on the government. In Canada, we are lucky to have a full range of human rights. Citizens in some other countries are not as fortunate. Human rights are often denied to any person or group that is labelled "different," including women, children, racial or ethnic minorities, people with mental or physical disabilities, and those whose belief, religion, or lifestyle is considered a threat by a majority group. Even governments that have laws and institutions to protect freedoms sometimes choose not to enforce them equally for all citizens.

Human Rights in Question

Maher Arar is a Canadian citizen of Syrian descent who was taken from a flight in New York City by American authorities. They suspected him of having ties to terrorist organizations in the Middle East. Although he was a Canadian citizen, carrying a Canadian passport, U.S. authorities deported him to Syria, where he was jailed for nearly a year. During that time, he claimed he was tortured into making a false confession.

American forces deported Arar to Syria in clear violation of his rights as a Canadian citizen. He has accused the Canadian government of failing to help him. A government inquiry ended in September 2005 after more than four months of hearings. The inquiry examined Arar's claims and confirmed that he had been tortured in Syria.

Questions

1. A Canadian passport is an important document. Research the rights it is supposed to guarantee and report to your class.

2. Use the WebLink below and research the Arar case. Make a list of the rights Arar claimed were violated.

◀ Maher Arar is a Syrian-born Canadian citizen who was deported from the United States to Syria, where he was tortured.

 Web Links

Information on the Arar Commission
To learn more about the inquiry and the final report of the Arar Commission, go to
www.nelson.com/civicsnow.

The United Nations

The international human rights struggle is an attempt to get people and governments to agree that each person in the world has worth and deserves the same rights and opportunities. The United Nations (UN) is one of the leading organizations that tries to protect and promote human rights internationally. After the horrors of the Second World War in which 68 million people died, the United Nations was established to promote international cooperation.

The UN quickly recognized the need for a global set of human rights. It developed the *Universal Declaration of Human Rights* in 1948. Then, in 1989, it introduced the *Convention on the Rights of the Child.* Over the years, the UN has developed many other statements on human rights to express tolerance and respect for human dignity. The first step in protecting your own human rights and those of others is to read and understand the principles found in these important documents. In Section 4.9, starting on page 177, we will examine the role of the UN in world affairs in more detail.

UN Declarations and Conventions
To learn more about and the *Universal Declaration of Human Rights* and the *Convention on the Rights of the Child,* go to **www.nelson.com/civicsnow**.

Amnesty International

Amnesty International is one of the most effective human rights organizations in the world. Founded in 1961 by a British lawyer named Peter Benenson, Amnesty International is a Nobel Prize winning grassroots organization. Its members use non-violent means, such as letter-writing campaigns, to free political prisoners. Many have been detained for their beliefs or because of their ethnic origin, sex, colour, or language. These political prisoners have not used or advocated violence in their struggles.

▲ Irene Khan is the Secretary General of Amnesty International, a well-known human rights organization.

Persuasion

Amnesty International pushes governments for fast but fair trials for these prisoners. It also wants an end to the death penalty and the torture of prisoners. It investigates and campaigns for the end of **arbitrary** executions and "disappearances" of people presumed murdered by brutal and anti-democratic regimes.

Education and awareness are an important part of Amnesty International's mission. Often, when faced with a global outcry, embarrassed governments release prisoners and make reforms.

arbitrary: Chosen at random.

Women's Rights

Women everywhere are especially vulnerable to human rights violations. Some cultures view women as less valuable than men. Often, women are not paid the same as men for doing the same work. Frequently, they are forced to take low-paying, dead-end jobs. Women are often not given the same opportunities to participate equally in education or politics.

Many cultures do not allow women to get an education or have a career. In some parts of the world, girls are forced into arranged marriages at a young age. In some cultures, women are physically harmed or even killed over dowries—the money or property the bride brings to her husband on marriage.

There are many human rights issues that affect women. There are human rights organizations dedicated to equality between women and men. They continue to struggle to change sexist attitudes. Their goal is to ensure that all men and women have the same rights, protections, and opportunities.

Civics Now DVD

"Half of the Sky: Women in China" from *Civics Now DVD*.

Literacy Strategy

While viewing the video clip on the DVD, make a connection between what you have learned and what you are viewing. Jot down your ideas and be prepared to justify your opinions.

↔ Check Your Understanding

1. In your own words, define human rights.
2. What significance does human rights have for individual citizens?
3. List 10 ways that human rights are abused or denied in various countries, including Canada.
4. List four choices that you can make in your daily activities to promote human rights at home and internationally.

Angelina Atyam and Graca Machel

Angelina Atyam, a Ugandan nurse, is one of the founders of the Concerned Parents Association. This is a group set up by parents of children abducted and forced to fight in local wars. Atyam began the organization after her 14-year-old daughter, Charlotte, was kidnapped in 1996 by a rebel group in northern Uganda. Since that time, Atyam has worked to try to free the children held captive by the rebels. In 2004, Charlotte was returned to her family, eight years after her kidnapping.

Atyam wants to let the world know about the problem of kidnapping as well as about the rights of children during military conflict. In 1998, Atyam was awarded the human rights prize by the United Nations. In 2002, she addressed the United Nations.

▲ Angelina Atyam founded Concerned Parents Association after her teenage daughter was kidnapped by Ugandan rebels.

Graca Machel is a crusader for children's rights. In 1975, she became the first minister of education in the newly independent Mozambique in Africa. Within 10 years, school enrolment doubled to over 80 percent of school-aged children. She had a lot of experience in teaching and dealing with children, so, in 1994, the United Nations chose her to write the report on the impact of armed conflict on children.

She helped many widows and orphans over the years. Through her UN work, she met another human rights advocate, Nelson Mandela, the former president of South Africa. They were married in 1998.

▲ Graca Machel is an internationally recognized advocate of children's rights.

Questions

1. What event turned Angelina Atyam into an active citizen?
2. Describe why Graca Machel is considered a champion of children's rights.

Web Links

Racism. Stop It! Campaign
To learn more about this Canadian educational and human rights campaign, go to **www.nelson.com/civicsnow**.

4.5 War and Armed Conflict

Focus Question

- *How are conflict resolution and peace linked?*

The Doomsday Clock

The Doomsday Clock, which is the symbol of the nuclear danger facing the world, was moved from nine to seven minutes to midnight on February 27, 2002. To find out the current setting of the Doomsday Clock, go to **www.nelson.com/civicsnow**.

As you can see from the world map on page 161, there is conflict in almost every part of the globe. Many of these are local fights, and some are civil wars between different groups in the same country. All violent conflict affects others, but a gun or missile on the other side of the world seems less threatening to us than one in our own backyard. However, this is not true of one type of weapon. Nuclear weapons can be launched from long-range bombers or from guided missiles from the other side of the globe. As such, they are a threat to every person on the planet.

Many nations have nuclear weapons or are able to make them. There are enough nuclear weapons in the world today to destroy all life on the planet. This source of mass destruction remains a grave threat to the survival of our species.

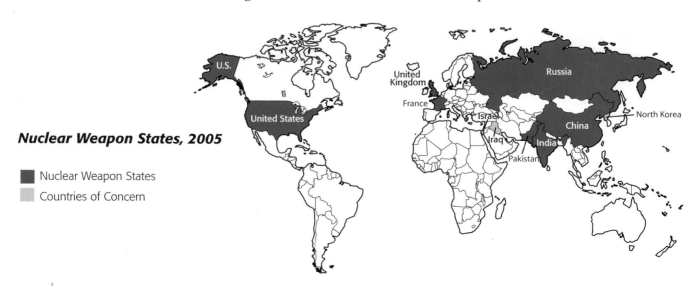

Nuclear Weapon States, 2005

■ Nuclear Weapon States
▨ Countries of Concern

In the search for peace, every person must devote himself or herself to the prevention of violent conflicts. The many causes of violent behaviour are complex; however, it is clear that most people do not know how to resolve conflicts peacefully. If we are to make a change in our communities, one effective strategy to reduce violence would be to train everyone in conflict resolution skills and teach violence prevention in our schools.

Wars and Armed Conflicts, 2005

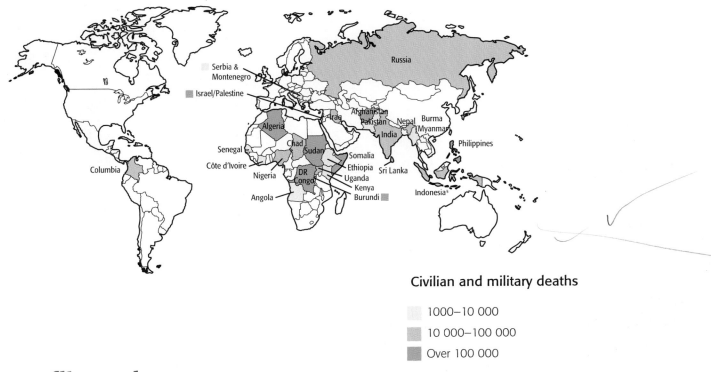

Civilian and military deaths

1000–10 000

10 000–100 000

Over 100 000

Conflict Today

Between 1989 and 2005, there were over 100 armed conflicts in the world. As of mid-2005, there were eight major wars under way, with as many as 24 lesser conflicts ongoing. (The UN defines a major war as a conflict that results in 1000 deaths per year.) Africa alone has faced 20 major civil wars since 1960.

Many of these conflicts last a long time. Since 1996, 60 percent of world conflicts have lasted more than five years, and one-third have lasted longer than 20 years. The majority of these conflicts are civil wars that occur within individual states. These ongoing hostilities are often ignored by the news media until they erupt into spectacular (and newsworthy) violence.

Cause of Conflicts

Individuals and groups have been disagreeing since the beginning of time. All too often, people resort to violence to settle their differences. Your teachers discourage you from using your fists to settle arguments in the classroom or schoolyard. In the same way, international organizations, such as the United Nations, try to convince nations and groups within nations to talk things out rather than fight.

▶ Members of the United Nations meet to find solutions and try to avoid conflict.

Money is often a reason for war. Land and resources such as minerals, forests, water, and so on are valuable. If one group owns them, another may try to take them away through violence.

Other causes of war include the struggle for more democratic government and law, the declaration of independent nation-states, and hatred between racial, ethnic, or religious groups.

Waging War

The mainstream media pay a lot of attention to high-tech weapons, such as "smart bombs" (laser-guided missiles), and discuss these in great detail. But, in reality, the weapons of choice in most armed conflicts are the traditional low-tech weapons such as knives, guns, grenades, and land mines. They are inexpensive and easy to obtain.

Weapons Manufacturing

Weapons manufacturing—both low-tech and high-tech—is a multibillion-dollar industry worldwide. Many nations and hundreds of industries get rich by exporting arms to war-torn areas. An international movement to oppose the spread of small arms and light weapons has begun. Those who profit have used their strong political and economic interests to defy the opposition.

Enforcing Peace: UN Peacekeeping

In 1956, the United Nations created a peacekeeping body known as the United Nations Emergency Force (UNEF) made up of soldiers from several member states. Its goal was to keep the fighters in the Middle East apart until a peace agreement was signed. The person who came up with the idea of using UN peacekeepers to stop fighting was Canadian diplomat and future prime minister, Lester Pearson. For his brilliant idea of international peacekeeping, he was awarded the Nobel Peace Prize in 1957. Since that time, the UN has dispatched UNEF forces around the world. The UN does not have an army, so member states volunteer troops and equipment. They are paid for this from a special peacekeeping budget.

▲ Prime Minister Pearson won the Nobel Peace Prize in 1957.

Establishing a Peacekeeping Force

Peacekeepers are lightly armed for self-defence. They rely on persuasion and minimal use of force to reduce tensions and prevent fighting. The success of peacekeeping efforts depends on the cooperation of the opposing sides. It is a dangerous business. Over 2000 UN military and civilian peacekeepers from over 100 countries have died while on duty. In 2005, 82 000 UN peacekeepers were involved in 17 peacekeeping operations.

▲ Canada has always played an important role in UN peacekeeping, such as this mission in Pakistan.

Peacekeeping Costs

Peacekeeping is expensive. The cost of UN peacekeeping in 2005 and 2006 will peak at $5 billion. All member states are obliged to pay their share of peacekeeping costs under an agreed-upon formula.

Peacekeeping Failures

UN peacekeepers are now asked to become peacemakers. This sometimes involves going into areas to stop violence without the agreement of the sides that are fighting. It is dangerous enough to get between two warring groups at their request, but when you go without being asked, it is particularly hazardous. Often, UN peacemakers have not been given the means to carry out some of their missions. The combination of many complex problems has resulted in failed peacemaking missions such as in Bosnia, Herzegovina, Rwanda, Somalia, Kosovo, and the Democratic Republic of the Congo. Canadian Roméo Dallaire led the failed UN mission in 1994 in Rwanda. (See his biography on page 186.)

Let's Discuss

Jawaharlal Nehru, the first prime minister of India, said that every aggressor claims to be acting on the defensive. This is also true of individuals. Have you personally experienced or witnessed aggression by others? Did any of these hostile people claim to be acting in self-defence?

The Cost of War

Many nations use a large percentage of their yearly budgets on military spending. Some citizens of these nations argue that this money is well spent protecting them from foreign and internal threats. Other citizens feel that military spending is too high. They believe that the money spent on military goods, such as weapons, could be better used for other things.

▲ Billions of dollars have been spent on military weapons, such as this fighter plane.

Below is a list of statistics that show the cost of war. If you could eliminate several of the costs in the list below, how would you use the money to better the world?

- Canadian exports of military goods totalled over $1 billion (Canadian) in 2004. Canada was ranked number six among global arms exporters.
- The U.S. has spent a minimum of $4 trillion on nuclear weapons since 1940.
- The cost of one B2 bomber is $100 million.
- The U.S. defence budget in 2006 is $442 billion, not including the wars in Afghanistan and Iraq. In the same year, the U.S. is spending $31 billion on education, $30 billion on children's health, $21 billion on affordable housing, and $7 billion on environmental protection agencies.

Global Arms Exports, 2004

Rank	Country	Billions $US
1	United States	18.6
2	Russia	4.6
3	France	4.4
4	United Kingdom	1.9
5	Germany	0.9
6	Canada	0.9
7	China	0.7
8	Israel	0.5

The End of War

Conflict resolution, along with humanitarian assistance and tools such as mediation, are needed to build a peaceful world. Without peace, we cannot have security and stability because they are only possible in peaceful conditions. Without these, other fundamental goals of global improvement cannot succeed. These include ending world hunger, improving the world's health, helping those in need, and spreading human rights.

Civics Now DVD

"Mapping Mozambique" from *Civics Now DVD*.

▶ Canadian volunteers help to rebuild homes hit by a tsunami in Thailand in late 2004.

↔ Check Your Understanding

1. Many of the casualties in modern wars and conflicts have been civilians. Why do you think this is?

2. What do you think is the biggest cause of war? Give examples. What are three other causes?

3. What are low-tech weapons? What are high-tech weapons?

4. Describe the role of a UN peacekeeper.

5. How does a UN peacekeeper differ from a "regular" soldier?

6. What problems do UN peacekeepers face in their missions?

7. State two arguments in support of military spending. State two arguments against military spending.

4.6 Environmental Citizenship

Focus Question

• *What is an environmental citizen?*

Environmental citizens are people who are aware of the environment and the damage we are doing to it. They recognize the fact that we are using up the natural resources that we rely on at a faster rate than nature can renew them. People are concerned about the natural world. They want to use resources so that they are not used up. They live and work in ways that pollute as little as possible. This is known as sustainable development, or **sustainability**.

▲ Recycling helps the environment.

Reduce, Reuse, and Recycle

Environmental citizens help the Earth in many ways. At home, at school, and in our community, people have decided to make a positive difference. One of the most famous environmental slogans is reduce, reuse, recycle.

The next time you start to do research for a school report, think of the three Rs. Reduce the amount of paper you use by making notes on both sides. Instead of printing out several versions of your report, correct it on screen and print out just the final version. Reuse paper by making notes on the back side of scrap paper. Finally, recycle by putting your used paper in the blue box. Also, remember to buy paper that has been recycled from used paper.

Civics Now DVD

"Temagami"
from *Civics Now DVD*.

Ecological Footprints

William Rees and Mathis Wackernagel created a way to measure and compare the environmental impact of people, cities, and nations around the world. In 1993, at the University of British Columbia, they coined the phrase "ecological footprint" as a metaphor for how our activity has an impact on the natural world. The ecological footprint measures how much land and water area any group requires to produce the resources it consumes and to absorb its wastes. The average Canadian footprint in 2005 is 8.6 hectares per person, the third highest in the world. The world average is 2.2 hectares. Understanding the impact we have on the environment can help us find ways to reduce that impact, and maintain less damaging habits.

Toronto's Average Footprint

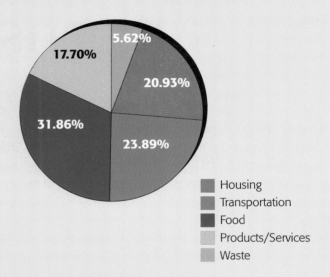

- Housing
- Transportation
- Food
- Products/Services
- Waste

Toronto's average ecological footprint is 5.3 hectares. That is quite a bit better than the Canadian average of 8.6, but not as good as the global average of 2.2.

 Web Links

Your Ecological Footprint
To learn more about ecological footprints, go to www.nelson.com/civicsnow.

Questions

1. List three things we can do to reduce our ecological footprint.

2. Canada's ecological footprint of 8.6 is the third-highest in the world. List three reasons why Canadians require so much land and water resources. Suggest three ways we could reduce this.

3. What does the pie chart tell us about people in Toronto?

↔ Check Your Understanding

1. List five things you could do to make yourself a better environmental citizen.

2. Reduce, Reuse, Recycle is one of the most famous environmental slogans. List three ways you can do each "R." Compare your answers with the class.

Bob Hunter

Bob Hunter felt strongly about protecting whales. He risked his life by putting himself between the giant animals and the harpoons of the hunters who were trying to kill them. Hunter was the co-founder of one of the leading environmental groups in the world—Greenpeace. The group was founded in Vancouver in 1971 by Hunter and other activists. They wanted to use creative but non-violent methods to get people's attention for their causes. These "creative confrontations" have included

- embarrassing companies that use trees from ancient forests for their products by making consumers aware of their actions
- encouraging teens to buy books and other paper products from companies that use recycled paper
- hanging enormous banners on oil refineries, nuclear power plants, and chemical manufacturers to draw attention to environmental change
- hosting explorations in various Arctic regions to document climate change
- using small boats to prevent the killing of whales, seals, overfishing, and nuclear testing

Before his death in 2005, Hunter won the 1994 Canadian Environmental Award.

▲ Bob Hunter was one of the founders of Greenpeace, one of the most well known environmental groups in the world.

Question

Research Greenpeace and other ecological groups, and report back to the class on three ways they have made a difference to the environment.

4.7 | The Indigenous Citizen

Focus Question

- *What challenges face the world's indigenous people?*

The Original People

Indigenous people are the original people to live in a region or country. Historically, their cultures have been overturned and their land has been **annexed** by people from other lands. Today, approximately 5000 indigenous cultures in the world include over 300 million people (see map on page 171). These cultures are quickly vanishing, which means that global **diversity** is declining. That is why the UN declared the International Decade of the World's Indigenous People (1995–2004) to recognize the many contributions of indigenous cultures.

annexed: To take over territory and make it part of another state.

diversity: A variety of people, cultures, beliefs, and so on.

Marginalized

Indigenous people have frequently been marginalized and mistreated in the past by the government and citizens of the groups that colonized them. They often were not granted full citizenship rights by settler societies. They continue to be a minority voice in their countries.

Basic Concerns

Indigenous people share two basic concerns:

1. how to maintain their cultural identities
2. how to control their own futures

▲ This is a Navajo Nation Council Chamber meeting.

Often they also want to regain their ancestral lands. This could provide them with more access to resources that would give them economic independence. They also want political freedoms and human rights.

Compromise

Some indigenous groups and some national governments are striving to reach a compromise. Some indigenous people want to form their own governments based on their beliefs and traditions. Beliefs may include things such as living in harmony with nature. Traditions may include making decisions by consensus or general agreement. Many Aboriginal peoples in Canada have become more self-governing (see pages 109–127).

Indigenous People of the World

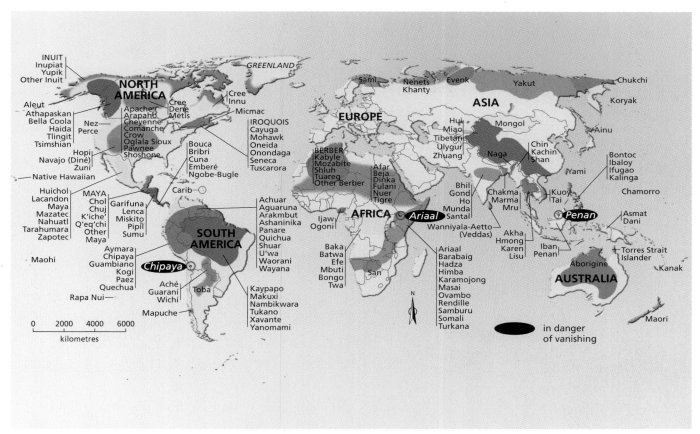

▲ This map shows some of the 5000 indigenous cultures throughout the world today. There are over 300 million indigenous people in the world.

Sandra Lovelace

Sandra Lovelace, a Maliseet from New Brunswick, filed a complaint with the UN Human Rights Committee in 1977 over the loss of her Indian status because she married a non-status man. In a similar situation, a First Nations man who had Indian status would not have lost his status under this law. The law assumed that the male was the head of the household. With the loss of her Indian status, Lovelace no longer had access to federal programs and benefits such as housing, education, and health care. Also, she could no longer live on the reserve.

The UN committee supported Lovelace and her case. Eventually, in 1985, the Canadian government amended the *Indian Act*, allowing any Aboriginal woman who married a non-status Indian or a non-Aboriginal man to maintain her Indian status. Mary Two-Axe Early, a Mohawk woman, was also key in pressuring the Canadian government to change its laws. She was the first Aboriginal woman to get her right to vote back—known as being **reenfranchised**—after losing her Indian status through marriage to a non-Aboriginal man.

▲ Sandra Lovelace took her battle for First Nations women's rights to the UN. She won.

Question

To get equality for Aboriginal women in Canada, why did Sandra Lovelace have to go to the United Nations?

↔ Check Your Understanding

Web Links

UN Declaration on the Rights of Indigenous People
To find out more about the *UN Declaration on the Rights of Indigenous People,* go to **www.nelson.com/civicsnow**.

1. Use the Web Links to the left to access the *UN Declaration on the Rights of Indigenous People.* List three key points in your own words.

2. Predict two potential issues arising from the affirmation of indigenous rights.

3. What challenges do indigenous people face in maintaining these rights?

4.8 | Protecting Democratic Rights

Focus Question

- *When are certain forms of political protest warranted and useful?*

Democratic Debate

Democracy is a system that allows and depends on vigorous debate, discussion, and consensus-building.

As a Canadian citizen:

- Can you be imprisoned for criticizing a government leader?
- Can you be denied the right to vote because of ethnicity, gender, or culture?
- Can you be forced to meet secretly in order to practise your religion or discuss ideas?

The answers to these questions are "No" for most Canadian citizens. But there are many countries where you could be imprisoned, denied the vote, or forced to meet secretly. Fortunately, Canadians are protected from such harsh treatment. Our rights as Canadian citizens are outlined in the *Canadian Charter of Rights and Freedoms.*

Democratic nations are supposed to encourage citizens to be independent. At least citizens are allowed to question the principles and practices of democracy. They have the right to protest peacefully the policies of their government or the actions of other groups.

They can protest by creating art, writing letters, distributing pamphlets, participating in demonstrations, and taking other forms of direct, legal citizen action.

▲ These people are participating in a peaceful protest against low welfare rates.

Peaceful Protest

Direct action, such as a public protest, is the right of everyone in a democracy. Protest is often used by groups that feel left out and believe they have no other way of being heard. Protests are a test of any democracy. They should be considered a place where diverse voices can be heard and considered.

Sometimes protests become too unruly and turn violent. Then the state has the right to protect its citizens and their property. The challenge for democratic governments is to balance citizens' right to safety with citizens' right to expression.

▲ This is an example of a peaceful anti-sweatshop protest staged in Greece and Australia before the 2004 Olympics.

Human Rights Defenders

Most defenders of human rights are ordinary people, not extraordinary leaders. They see that something is wrong and try to correct it. Significant change in our world occurs at the community level.

Suppose the provincial government wanted to close your school because of declining enrolment and sell it to a developer. How could you influence this decision and save your school? Why might you decide to do so? Such changes are often not reported in great detail by the media. Public figures, such as politicians, generally want to keep everybody happy and will not get involved unless someone complains. However, the dedication of people to causes that they believe in can bring about change in schools, neighbourhoods, countries, and the world.

Methods of Non-violent Action

When citizens cooperate in groups, the possibilities for change are often stronger. Peaceful, non-violent, democratic protests take place in most parts of the world. Here are some of the ways that global citizens can promote awareness of their views and their desire for action:

- Write a letter of opposition (or support) to an editor, politician, businessperson, or member of the media.
- Create a Weblog that outlines your beliefs on an issue and connects others to important places to gain information and take action.
- Create a **petition** calling for specific changes that you would like to see take place, collect signatures, and send it to someone who can make those changes take place.
- Participate in a community/council meeting.
- Create a banner, song, symbol, play, children's book, cartoon, computer game, or piece of artwork, and share it with other people.
- Hold a **vigil** or a mock trial.
- Organize a fundraiser for a group that supports something you believe in.
- Lobby a committee or group.
- Organize an assembly of protest or support, or a teach-in, boycott, sit-in, or pray-in.
- Join an NGO, political party, community, or cultural group.
- Boycott products.

Let's Discuss

Which methods of non-violent action do you think are the most effective in promoting democratic change? Which methods of non-violent action would you be willing to use? Under what conditions would you be willing to use them?

petition: A formal written request signed by many people.

vigil: A solemn meditation, prayer, or talk by a group of people, usually at night.

Web Links

Getting Together for Change
To learn more about Canadian groups and organizations that are involved in direct action for change, go to **www.nelson.com/civicsnow**.

◀ Candlelight vigils, like this one in Ottawa, are popular methods of non-violent action.

Difference

Nelson Mandela

As a result of fighting the racist policies of South Africa, Nelson Mandela was sentenced to life imprisonment in 1962. While in prison he continued to work against human rights violations. After much pressure at home and around the world, he was released from prison in 1990. From being a prisoner in his own country to becoming its elected president in 1994, Nelson Mandela's internationally recognized heroism led to his winning the Nobel Peace Prize in 1993.

▲ Nelson Mandela is one of the best known human rights defenders.

Question

1. How do you think citizens of other countries could have put pressure on the South African government to release Mandela from prison and end the racism?

2. The South African government tried to silence Mandela by imprisoning him. What other methods might a government use against those who speak out in opposition?

Let's Discuss

Nelson Mandela said, "The overwhelming majority of South Africans will always be indebted to the people of Canada for their solidarity with us in the long, dark years of our struggle for freedom. We hold in the highest esteem Canada's lasting tradition of dedication to human rights." In what ways is Canada worthy of Mr. Mandela's praise? Is Canada a good global citizen? In what ways could Canada improve?

↔ *Check Your Understanding*

1. When do democratic governments have the right to stop protests? Give examples.

2. Why should a variety of opinions be encouraged in a democracy?

3. Democratic governments have to balance citizens' right to safety with citizens' right to expression. Think of a contemporary example of a provincial, federal, or global government attempting to achieve this balance and assess its actions.

4. List four of the best methods of non-violent action that promote democracy. Provide examples of two that you have heard of in your community or the news. Were the actions successful? Why or why not?

4.9 | The United Nations

Focus Question

- *How does the UN promote the rights and responsibilities of global citizenship?*

Once you have worked together with others, you soon understand how hard it is to do anything that satisfies everyone. It is hard to get your friends to agree on something relatively simple, such as what movie to see or what to eat for lunch. Imagine how difficult it must be to get the nations of the world—with their vastly different needs, resources, and populations—to cooperate. That is what the United Nations tries to do.

▲ The United Nations logo on its flag represents the continents of the world, surrounded by olive branches, the symbol for peace.

International Cooperation

People have dreamed for a long time about an international organization that would maintain world peace, human rights, and justice for everyone. In 1945, after millions had died in two World Wars, this dream finally became a reality. National leaders met and discussed this new global partnership. Before this, countries had cooperated on such things as international mail and communications, but in limited ways. On October 24, 1945, 51 countries signed the *Charter of the United Nations.* Today, 191 nations are members, which is almost every nation in the world.

According to the *Charter,* signed in 1945, the UN has four purposes:

1. to maintain international peace and security
2. to develop friendly relations among nations
3. to cooperate in solving international problems and in promoting respect for human rights
4. to be a centre for harmonizing the actions of nations

Let's Discuss

UN Secretary General Kofi Annan said, "Together we are the ultimate power. If we pull our efforts together, we can get almost everything done—all of us around the world—'We the People.'" Do you agree with Kofi Annan's definition of power? Why or why not?

Civics Now DVD

"Kosovo"
from *Civics Now DVD.*

How the UN is Organized

The UN is not a world government. It does not make laws for all nations. Instead, it tries to resolve conflicts and tries to get its members to agree on ideas and actions. The UN Assembly cannot force any state to take action. It has influence rather than power. Its opinions and advice often reflect world opinion and often represent what the global community believes is right. In 2004, the UN's regular budget (which doesn't cover any peacekeeping missions) amounted to some $1.48 billion.

The United Nations has four main parts based at UN headquarters in New York City. (Another part of the UN, the international courts, are based in The Hague in the Netherlands–see pages 182-187). The four parts are

1. the General Assembly
2. the Security Council
3. the Economic and Social Council
4. the Secretary General and the Secretariat

▲ The United Nations building in New York City.

Parts of the United Nations

The General Assembly

Each member nation has five delegates who sit in the General Assembly. Each nation has one vote, and any act or agreement is passed with a two-thirds majority.

The Assembly decides on international activities, such as peacekeeping or disaster relief. Debating and working in committees takes up a lot of time in the General Assembly.

The Security Council

The Security Council's main duty is to maintain world peace. It is the only part of the UN that can make decisions that member states have to follow. The Security Council has 15 members. Five are permanent members, and the other 10 are elected for two-year terms. Canada has served six two-year terms, more than any other non-permanent member nation.

The five permanent members of the Security Council are

- China
- France
- the Russian Federation
- the United Kingdom
- the United States

The permanent members have the right to veto—or reject—any vote made in the Council. The UN is discussing ways to improve the Security Council.

Years Canada Participated on the UN Security Council

1948–1949
1958–1959
1967–1968
1977–1978
1989–1990
1999–2000

A Year at a Glance: The 2004–2005 Session of the UN General Assembly

Agenda Items
There are over 200 different topics in total.

- peace and security issues
- protection of the environment worldwide
- emergency assistance to victims of earthquakes and floods
- promotion of international trade
- worldwide campaign to fight AIDS, tuberculosis, and malaria
- disarmament (nuclear weapons, landmines)
- development of poorer nations
- child and adolescent mental health
- reform toward the improvement of the UN

The Economic and Social Council

The Economic and Social Council (ECOSOC) of the UN oversees areas such as education, economics, health, and human rights. It is made up of 54 members. Each year, 18 members are elected for three-year terms, ensuring constant rotation.

The UN's Purpose
To learn more about the United Nations, go to
www.nelson.com/civicsnow.

▲ Secretary General Kofi Annan at the United Nations.

Literacy Strategy

If you are unsure about the meaning of certain words, think of a word that is similar, such as a root word, and read it in context. Sometimes its meaning will be slightly different than what you think depending on the context.

UN Issues

To learn more about the United Nations and how to create your own model United Nations at your school, go to www.nelson.com/civicsnow.

The Secretary General and the Secretariat

At the heart of the United Nations organization is the Secretary General and the Secretariat, or permanent staff who run the day-to-day operations of the UN. The Secretariat has a staff of nearly 9000 from 170 different countries. The UN has offices around the world, from Addis Ababa to Vienna.

The secretary general is the head of the UN. He is elected for a five-year term by the General Assembly. The present secretary general is Kofi Annan. He is the seventh person to hold this office since the UN was founded in 1945.

United Nations Branches

The UN has formed special groups for many areas of human need. These special groups include 50 committees and working groups that report to the General Assembly. Here is a partial list of the organizations that are joined to the UN through special agreements:

International Labour Organization (ILO)

- to improve working conditions and set labour standards to be used by countries around the world

Food and Agriculture Organization of the UN (FAO)

- to improve living standards by improving agricultural methods and education

UN Educational, Scientific, and Cultural Organization (UNESCO)

- promotes education for all, cultural development, protection of the world's natural and cultural heritage, international cooperation in science, press freedom, and communication

World Health Organization (WHO)

- coordinates programs to solve health problems such as immunization and health education

The World Bank

- to reduce world poverty by providing loans and technical assistance to developing countries

Speaking Out!

Is the UN Really Working?

"The UN is expensive and wasteful. They have all those meetings, committees, and employees that don't seem to amount to much. We live in a violent world, in which most people remain poor. The UN seems to be controlled by rich nations like those represented on the Security Council. Why should they get more say than the others by using their veto power? In the General Assembly, small nations can outvote the rest of the nations of the world.

The 12 largest nations in terms of population, like China, India, and the United States, only have 12 votes out of 191. How is that fair? Sure, some peacekeeping missions may be successful but I think that you should leave countries to figure out their own problems. Many UN members don't even listen to the UN anymore. They simply sign agreements and conventions and then refuse to implement them. What's the point of that?"

"The UN doesn't claim to be perfect. It actually encourages many groups to monitor its successes and failures in order to change the UN for the better. Trying to keep peace, maintain human rights, promote environmental health, and assist developing nations is not an easy job. The UN brings the problems to the world's attention. This is one of the most important ways to get people to think about solutions to the problems.

The UN has had many successes. It has saved millions of people from becoming casualties of war. It has negotiated 172 peaceful settlements to regional conflicts. It has enabled democratic elections in over 45 countries. It has promoted development in hundreds of countries and promoted human rights worldwide. Protecting the environment through treaties and minimizing the threat of nuclear war are just some of the achievements of the UN. The money it costs the nations of the world to support the UN is a fraction of the costs of war, poverty, and ignorance. The UN is one of the best ways to improve our world."

Questions

1. Identify the viewpoints of the two speakers.

2. What evidence do they provide to support their opinions?

3. Which speaker do you think has the stronger argument and why?

◀ These women are voting in an Afghan election. The woman on the left is a UN observer.

International Law and Justice

Every nation has its own government and laws. If a Canadian citizen commits a crime in, say, France, that person is tried under French law in French courts even though they are not French citizens. But what about nations? Can they be taken to court? Do global laws and courts exist?

International Laws and Agreements

One of the UN's functions is to help develop laws that all nations of the world can follow. There are a lot of international laws and agreements. However, any given international law, such as a convention, treaty, or set of standards, binds only countries that agree to it. The UN does not have the power to enforce international laws.

Examples of Areas of International Law Based on UN Conventions and Agreements

- diplomatic relations (how host countries should treat ambassadors and staff)
- the use of international waterways
- protection for people with no country
- protection of oceans from pollution, allowing navigation, research, and equal access by all countries
- treaties against drug trafficking
- rules and guidelines to help regulate international trade
- international environmental protection against deforestation, damaging the ozone layer, and regulating the movement of hazardous wastes
- international agreements against terrorism
- humanitarian law (the *Convention on Genocide*, the *Universal Declaration of Human Rights*, and so on)
- new laws to deal with outer space (which countries should control discoveries in space?)

▲ The UN Office of Outer Space Affairs (UNOOSA) promotes international cooperation in the peaceful uses of outer space. It trains people in subjects such as basic space science, satellite navigation, search and rescue, and space law.

Let's Discuss

The years 1990 to 1999 were named the United Nations Decade of International Law, in hopes of promoting the role of the UN court. The years 2003 to 2012 are named the United Nations Literacy Decade, to promote the idea of "literacy as freedom." What worthy global cause do you think the UN should proclaim for the next decade?

The UN International Court of Justice

When UN members violate international law, they may have to explain themselves before the UN International Court of Justice. The court consists of 15 judges, who serve nine-year terms. They come from all parts of the world and from different legal systems. Since its founding in 1946, the court has made fewer than 90 judgments. Most countries are reluctant to take their disputes there because they don't want their governments to be held accountable to an authority outside of their own nations.

▲ The International Court of Justice in The Hague, Netherlands.

Cases Before the Court

The following cases were in the process of hearings or deliberations at the International Court of Justice in 2005:

- Democratic Republic of the Congo versus Rwanda (concerning armed conflict on the Territory of the Congo)
- Democratic Republic of the Congo versus Uganda (concerning armed conflict on the Territory of the Congo)

The following cases were pending, or waiting to be heard, before the court:

- Application of the *Convention on the Prevention and Punishment of the Crime of Genocide:* Bosnia and Herzegovina v. Serbia and Montenegro; Croatia v. Serbia and Montenegro
- Maritime and terrorist questions: Nicaragua v. Honduras; Nicaragua v. Colombia; Malaysia v. Singapore; Romania v. Ukraine

The Convention on Genocide, 1948

The mass murder of selected groups of people is known as **genocide**. It is an evil part of human history. Unfortunately, genocide is not just an unpleasant chapter of the world's history. Although it seems unbelievable, it still occurs in today's global village.

Following World War II, the German Nazi leaders were put on trial. The Nuremberg Trials (1945–1947) gave the world community its first chance to learn about the **Holocaust** and the crime of genocide. The Nazis had tried to kill off Jews and other "undesirables." The UN's *Convention on Genocide* (1948) finally defined genocide as a "crime against humanity" that must be prevented and punished.

Holocaust: The mass murder of Jews and other "undesirables" by the Nazis during World War II.

Civics Now DVD

"Auschwitz" from *Civics Now DVD*.

▲ German Nazi leaders (seated) were put on trial for war crimes at Nuremberg, 1945–1947.

The UN's Definition of Genocide

The UN defines genocide as acts that intend to destroy a national, ethnic, racial, or religious group. These include

- killing members of the group
- causing serious bodily or mental harm to members of the group
- deliberately inflicting on the group conditions of life calculated to bring about its physical destruction in whole or in part (that is, systematic starvation)
- imposing measures intended to prevent births within the group
- forcibly transferring children of the group to another group

Genocide

To learn more about genocide, go to **www.nelson.com/civicsnow**.

Genocides in the 20th Century

- *Dafur, Sudan 2003–2005: from 50 000 to 180 000 died; currently under investigation by International Criminal Court

- *Sierra Leone 1992–1999: over 10 000 deaths

- Rwanda 1994: more than 800 000 deaths

- Cambodia 1975–1979: 1.5 to 2.3 million deaths

- *East Timor 1975–1999: 100 000 to 250 000 deaths

- *Burundi 1993–1997: 150 000 to 200 000 deaths

- *Indonesia 1965–1966: 500 000 to 1 million

- The Nazi Holocaust 1938–1945: 9 to 11 million deaths

- Nanking 1937–1938: 130 000 to 300 000 deaths

- USSR-forced famine in the Ukraine 1932–1933: 3 to 10 million deaths

- Armenians in Turkey 1915–1919: 800 000 to 1.5 million deaths

*accurate statistics not available

UN International Tribunals

In 1994, during a civil war in the central African country of Rwanda, nearly a million Tutsis were murdered by the rival Hutus. That year, the UN Security Council set up a court, known as a tribunal, to look into accusations of genocide in Rwanda. Several people were tried for war crimes. In 1998, the Rwanda Tribunal became the first international court to hand down a verdict of genocide—the first-ever sentence for that crime.

Failure to Stop Genocide

The sad fact remains that the *Convention on Genocide* has not worked. Since the UN passed the *Convention* in 1948, hundreds of thousands of people have been brutally murdered. The international community has often failed to intervene in wars, or waited until it was too late to do anything useful. The people who committed the crimes are not held accountable. The barriers to ending genocide include nations not wanting to get involved with another nation's problems and their situations.

▲ This Tutsi woman is being held captive by Hutu militia in Rwanda, 1994.

Roméo Dallaire

Canadian Roméo Dallaire was named the Force Commander of the United Nations Assistance Mission for Rwanda in 1994. Nearly a million Rwandan Tutsis and moderate Hutus were killed in just 100 days—many by being hacked to death with machetes. This genocide was planned by the Rwandan government of extremist Hutus. General Dallaire had told the United Nations about the planned genocide. He also told them that he intended to seize the weapons that had been set aside for the killing.

In spite of all this, the United Nations forbade him from taking action. Dallaire repeated his appeal to the United Nations but with no success. Once the genocide began, Dallaire developed a plan to stop the killing, but the United Nations ordered him and his forces to prepare to leave the country. Dallaire refused. He helped to establish sanctuaries and saved the lives of tens of thousands of refugees.

In 2004, the UN secretary general admitted that the UN and the international community as a whole had failed Rwanda and could have acted together to avert the genocide. In 2003, Dallaire published his autobiography, *Shake Hands with the Devil.*

Questions

1. What qualities made Roméo Dallaire an exceptional global citizen?
2. What problems did he face in promoting human rights?
3. What lessons can be learned from the Rwandan genocide?

▶ Canadian General Roméo Dallaire was commander of the UN mission in Rwanda in 1994. He helped to save the lives of tens of thousands of refugees.

The International Criminal Court

It is one thing to have rules of war, but how do you enforce them? If war criminals can just ignore the law, what is the point in having rules? Punishing human rights' violators finally became possible in 1998. That year, 120 nations voted to establish an International Criminal Court (ICC). By doing this, the international community made it clear that human rights' violators and war criminals would no longer go unpunished. Some countries, including the United States, voted against having the court. They did not want their military personnel to be subject to the laws of an international court system.

The ICC is located in The Hague, the Netherlands. It has 18 internationally respected judges elected for a nine-year term as well as prosecutors and investigators. It hears cases of the most serious crimes of international concern: genocide, crimes against humanity, and war crimes.

▲ These judges in the International Criminal Court in the Netherlands hear cases of the most serious international crimes.

In 2005, the International Criminal Court was investigating three situations:

1. the Sudan, where about 180 000 people have died in Dafur through violence, starvation, and disease, since a rebel uprising began in early 2003

2. the Republic of Uganda, where a civic conflict that began in 1986 has seen the use of child soldiers, the rape of civilians, and the looting of villages

3. the Democratic Republic of the Congo, where nearly 4 million people have died since 1998 from a civil conflict that involves many neighbouring countries

The International Criminal Court will be responsible for punishing the individuals found responsible for these crimes.

Let's Discuss

Russian dictator Joseph Stalin once said, "A single death is a tragedy, a million deaths is a statistic." Discuss this quotation. Create a presentation that inspires awareness and caring in people about the issue of genocide or an example of genocide. Write to a consulate regarding your concerns about a current or potential genocide in that consulate's country.

What Can I Do?

You have learned a lot about human rights' abuses and war crimes in conflicts around the world. You have seen that the UN tries to prevent and end these tragedies but does not always get cooperation from others who do not share the same concerns.

The most effective way to prevent genocide and other crimes against humanity is to ensure that all people have basic human rights. You can help in this goal by believing in those rights and teaching them to others, living by them every day, and standing up for them when the opportunity presents itself. Individual people, not international courts and laws, are the key to global peace and human dignity.

▶ By working together, and by believing in human rights and standing up for them, young people can strive toward global peace.

↔ *Check Your Understanding*

1. What is the purpose of the UN?

2. What is the Security Council? How does it work?

3. How does the UN protect human rights?

4. Define genocide in your own words.

5. Why were the Nuremberg Trials a turning point in world history?

6. What significant measure did the UN's *Convention on Genocide* accomplish? Why was it an important step in international law?

7. Who is bound by international law?

8. Why are people like you the best defence against violations of human rights?

4.10 Canada's Role in the Global Community

Focus Question

• *What is Canada's role in the global community?*

From Lester Pearson to Roméo Dallaire, Canadians can find much to be proud of concerning our country's contribution to global issues. Canada has a unique position in the world. Geographically, we are situated between the United States and the Russian Federation. Our nation extends from the Pacific Ocean to the Atlantic Ocean.

We have important links with countries of the Pacific and with European nations. Our multicultural makeup gives us a variety of traditions and perspectives. Canada is a non-aggressive, mid-sized power with a tradition of peacekeeping and international mediation. Our economic prosperity, democratic government, and social programs are goals that many nations hope to attain.

Meet Canadian Heroes
To learn more about Canadians who are making positive changes in the world, go to **www.nelson.com/civicsnow**.

Canada and Its Neighbours

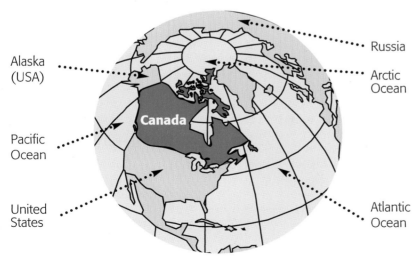

◀ Canada is located between the United States and the Russian Federation. We have coasts on the Arctic Ocean, the Pacific Ocean, and the Atlantic Ocean.

Making A Difference

Severn Cullis-Suzuki

At the age of 13, Vancouver native Severn Cullis-Suzuki won the 1993 Global 500 Award from the United Nations for her lifetime dedication to environmental issues. The previous year, she and three classmates raised money to go to the UN's Rio Earth Summit. At the Summit, she made a speech to the delegates. It was so popular that the UN made her a regular advisor on environmental issues. Cullis-Suzuki believes that Canadian youth need to take responsibility for how their lifestyles affect the global environment.

Questions

1. Cullis-Suzuki thinks your generation is disconnected from the natural world. Do you agree? Provide evidence for your answer.
2. What one action can you or your class take as global citizens, with a focus on the environment? Compare your answers and decide on which action to take.

▲ Severn Cullis-Suzuki is an advisor to the UN on environmental issues. She is the daughter of well-known environmental activist, David Suzuki.

Web Links

Signing on to a Sustainable Lifestyle

To learn more about Severn Cullis-Suzuki's "Recognition of Responsibility," which outlines specific actions that young people can take that support a more sustainable lifestyle, go to **www.nelson.com/civicsnow**.

Canada and the World

Here is a list of some of the international agreements and associations that reflect the Canadian government's involvement in world affairs:

- is a member of the G8—an economic alliance with the United States, Germany, France, Great Britain, Italy, Japan, and Russia

- has been involved in most UN peacekeeping missions

- gives millions of dollars in food aid

- provides military aid through the Department of National Defence—recent missions include Haiti, Kosovo, and Afghanistan

- has a military alliance with the United States in the North American Aerospace Defense Command (NORAD) for air and space surveillance and defence

- has a military alliance with 26 European nations in the North Atlantic Treaty Organization (NATO)

- is involved in free trade agreements with the United States and Mexico (North American Free Trade Agreement [NAFTA]), the Caribbean and Latin America (Free Trade Area of the Americas [FTAA])

- is a member of the Organization of American States (OAS), a group that discusses political and economic concerns

- has undertaken trading agreements with the European Union, Canada's second largest trading partner (the United States is Canada's largest trading partner)

- is a member of APEC, the Asia-Pacific Economic Cooperation

- is a member of the World Bank Organization

- is a member of the World Trade Organization (WTO), a group of over 148 nations that account for 90 percent of world trade, trying to encourage global free trade

- organizes aid worldwide with funds from the federal government and other NGOs in the Canadian International Development Agency (CIDA)

- accepts more immigrants in proportion to our population than any other nation in the world

- provides experts who are often sought as negotiators for peace by governments of other nations (that is, Ireland) and constitutional experts to help in the drafting of new democratic constitutions (that is, Afghanistan)

▲ This peacekeeper is delivering food to needy people. Providing aid around the world makes Canada a good global citizen.

The Future of Democratic Citizenship

The world has changed a great deal since the United Nations was founded in 1945. The original 50 founding members has grown to 191, nearly four times. Today, about two-thirds of the people in the world live in democratic societies. In these countries, all citizens can vote in elections and take part in the democratic process. This is a positive trend. However, just because a country has a democratic government does not necessarily mean that all citizens have full rights and freedoms. Sometimes decisions are made to satisfy the majority, and minorities may suffer.

The Future of Democracy

Democracy can survive only if governments, organizations, and individuals hear several points of view and consider them all before making decisions.

The future holds many challenges for citizens who believe in democracy. The formation of new democracies, nationalism, global economy, and technology may help democracy to develop or may inhibit it.

▲ Taking a vote in class, by a show of hands, is just one form of democracy in action.

New Democracies

Many nations are struggling to develop working democracies. The citizens of those nations that used to have non-democratic forms of government have to learn about the rights and responsibilities of democracy. Many people view democracy with suspicion. New democracies can be very fragile and are especially vulnerable to conflicts among their citizens. Will the new democracies of this decade become stable and prosperous nations?

▲ This is the Romanian Parliament. Romania is a new democracy.

Speaking Out!

Freedom and Security

"The real threat to democracy worldwide is terrorism. Radical groups want to destroy the way we live and want to intimidate us. Whatever it takes to protect our country and its citizens is all right by me. Our law enforcement officials should be allowed to listen in on phone conversations, search without warrants, and detain anyone they suspect of being a terrorist.

Keeping lists of people who belong to suspected terrorist organizations is a good idea, too. I would rather sleep at night not worried about terrorist attacks than concern myself about a loss of 'rights.' What good are the rights of citizens when you can't protect yourself from your enemies?"

"The war on terror has gone too far and has become a war on democracy. Terrorists are not stopped by taking away the rights of our citizens. I realize that it frightens people to think about terrorist attacks, but the government violating our civil rights is not the answer. The government's new *Anti-Terrorism Act* has the power to brand people as members of terrorist groups without convicting them of breaking laws.

Canadian citizens have been detained or imprisoned wrongfully because they are 'suspected terrorists.' We already have laws that protect us from criminals. We don't need new laws that compromise the freedoms we once had. If I end up living in a country where democratic rights are taken away due to fear, the terrorists have won by making us more autocratic!"

◀ Security officers were on alert at Pearson International Airport the day after the terrorist attacks in the Unted States on September 11, 2001.

Questions
1. In your own words, summarize the main argument of both speakers.
2. What evidence do they present to support their opinions?
3. Which speaker do you think has the stronger argument and why?

Civil Rights
To learn more about the civil rights of teenagers and all Canadian citizens, go to www.nelson.com/civicsnow.

Nationalism

Pride in your nation (even if the nation hasn't been recognized as independent) can be a unifying force in a community. However, it can also divide people. In any group, there are always some who think they are better than everyone else. The same is true of national groups. There are many examples of people who feel that their nation and culture are somehow better than others. Often, they act on these feelings of superiority in aggressive ways. This can result in violent acts, such as invading other countries or suppressing the rights of certain groups.

Global Citizenship

It is possible that citizens of the future will reject nationalism and see themselves less as part of a nation and more as part of the world—the global village. Perhaps the threat of an environmental or military disaster will force us to unite in an effort to save our planet.

The Global Economy

As we saw at the beginning of this unit, we are part of the global village. All communities and countries are more interconnected and interdependent. This is reflected in international economic agreements. These agreements have sometimes unified currencies, such as the 2001 introduction of the euro in the European Union. Others have stopped the use of taxes known as tariffs to protect one country's economy from foreign competition (e.g., the North American Free Trade Agreement).

▲ In 2001, the countries of the European Union replaced their old currencies with the euro.

Free Trade

Some people feel that free trade agreements benefit the countries involved by making economies more competitive and providing a wider choice of goods and services for people. Others have argued that free trade ensures that the most powerful economic nations dominate others in the agreement. Bankruptcies, layoffs of workers, and reduced wages may result as nations compete with one another.

◀ Some people think free trade is good for the global economy, while others disagree.

Multinational Corporations

Many people believe that the world benefits from increased international trade. They argue that more trade means more competition, which keeps prices down. At the same time, more trade means more jobs and more goods and services for more people. However, some wonder whether the **multinational corporations** that provide us with our goods might not have too much influence.

Business Profits

Like all businesses, multinational corporations aim to make as much money as they can for their shareholders. Often, in order to make greater profits, they are willing to take advantage of cheaper labour costs and lower environmental standards in developing countries. Will they respect the wants and needs of the particular communities in which they do business? Will they cooperate with or pressure governments to achieve their aims? Will they protect human rights? Will they protect the environment? Will they be accountable to the public or only to their own directors and shareholders?

Technology

Communications technology includes tools such as computers, cell phones, digital cameras, and many other high-tech items. How do these advances affect your ability to respond to areas of civic concern? Let's say that you have heard that city council wants to impose a 10:30 P.M. curfew on anyone under the age of 16. What can you do? Can you use the technology that you have in your campaign? Let's imagine that you have heard about horrible abuses of human rights that are occurring in another country. What can you do? Will technology assist you in becoming informed and taking action?

multinational corporations: Large business organizations based in one country that have multiple factories and offices in other countries.

▲ These people are working in a textile factory in Latin America. Some of the clothes you buy may have come from this factory.

◀ These young people are using cell-phone technology to communicate with others and to take action.

▲ Computer labs are common in schools today. This gives all students access to computers.

The Internet

Communication technologies such as the Internet are revolutionizing the amount of information that you can access and the speed at which you can find it. You no longer have to rely on news reports from Canada. You can access news and information worldwide, read viewpoints from different perspectives, and learn first-hand what conditions are like in other countries. The Internet seems like a wonderful tool for the global citizen, but, as with any tool, it can be abused and misused.

The World's Most Wired Nations

Top 15 Countries in Internet Usage		
Year-end 2004:	Internet Users (in millions)	Share %
1. United States	185.6	19.86
2. China	99.8	10.68
3. Japan	78.1	8.35
4. Germany	41.9	4.48
5. India	36.9	3.96
6. United Kingdom	33.1	3.54
7. South Korea	31.7	3.39
8. Italy	25.5	2.73
9. France	25.5	2.73
10. Brazil	22.3	2.39
11. Russia	21.2	2.27
12. Canada	20.5	2.19
13. Mexico	13.9	1.49
14. Spain	13.4	1.44
15. Australia	13.0	1.39
Top 15 Countries	662.4	70.88
Worldwide Total	934.5	100.00

Let's Discuss

Some people have suggested that the Canadian government should tax e-mail. Do you agree or disagree? Why or why not?

Access

What if you don't have access to a computer and the Internet? In your class, some students can use the Net at home to find the latest information for their civics projects, while others must rely on the school or local library facilities. What advantages are there to having access to the Net? The same question applies to Internet use worldwide. There will be "have" and "have-not" people, communities, and nations.

Privacy

With the use of technology, many people are concerned about the new ways that governments and businesses can gain information about us. The use of debit and credit cards, computer scanners in stores, and the Internet makes us more vulnerable to those who want to know who we are, what we eat, how much money we have, and other personal information that we want to keep private.

Social Isolation

Although technology may help to make us global citizens, the use of technology—hours of Internet searches, chats, and computer games—may further isolate us from direct contact with our neighbours and make us less likely to share in local concerns and to take action.

A Global Vision

Most people hope that the future will bring a peaceful world with economic, political, and human rights. Many share this vision. How will your own actions help to make this dream a reality? How will you become a good, informed, active, and global citizen?

↔ *Check Your Understanding*

1. Has the world changed in the past 50 years in terms of democracy? If so, how? Be prepared to defend your answer.
2. Define "global economy."
3. List one positive and one negative viewpoint about multinational corporations.
4. What positive role can communication technologies have in creating a better world?
5. In what ways is Canada a good global citizen? How can Canada be a better global citizen?
6. What do you think is the greatest challenge to the growth of world democracy?

▲ Technology, such as this debit card terminal, can threaten our privacy.

▲ You can become a good, informed, active, and global citizen.

Literacy Strategy

Use these questions as a guide to summarize the content. Read the questions and answer them carefully, referring to the notes that you made as you read. If you are not sure of the answers, reread the section and jot down the main ideas in your own words. Then return to these questions to complete the answers.

Skills for Social Action

Using Inquiry Skills to Study Civics Topics

A good method for analyzing and researching a topic in civics is the inquiry process. You begin by asking a meaningful question about the topic and this serves to guide your research. Suppose your topic is to investigate a proposed new federal law to lower the voting age to 16. These are the steps you could follow:

1. Formulate a question about the topic. It could be "Is lowering the voting age a positive step for democracy in Canada?"

2. Create an organizer similar to the one on this page.

3. Develop a number of criteria that allow you to come to a conclusion based on evidence. For example, a lower federal voting age would have a number of effects on Canada, which could be beneficial or not. Some of these effects would involve the cost of elections, issues identified as important during a campaign, and voter turnout and involvement. Write the criteria down the side of the page.

4. Find as much material as possible on the topic. Here you could use newspapers, articles in magazines or journals, research reports, or interviews you have had with concerned individuals. Use this information to fill in the organizer in point form.

5. When you have finished your research, look at both alternatives. Which one appears to have the strongest points?

6. Make a decision, answering your original question.

Criteria	Lower Voting Age to 16	Keep Voting Age at 18
Election costs		
Issues identified as important		
Voter turnout and involvement		
Other criteria		

How to Write a Research Report

A research report is a factual paper whose purpose is to describe a topic and present information clearly. Usually a research report attempts to answer a question, giving the reader enough background information to understand both the question and the answer. Follow these steps to write an effective research report.

1. Decide on a topic for your research report. Make sure you choose a topic that you are interested in—perhaps a civics issue that concerns you, a friend, or your family. Start by asking a question that is narrow enough to guide your research and broad enough to allow for deep investigation. For example, if you want to research the effects of lowering the voting age in Canada to 16, "Should Canada lower the voting age to 16?" might be too vague—it doesn't say what might be accomplished. "Would lowering the voting age to 16 strengthen democracy in Canada?" is a narrower focus that still allows for detailed research.

2. Identify the sources that will provide you with information for your report. Possible sources include

   - videos/DVDs
   - books, newspapers, and magazines
   - class notes
   - Web sites
   - radio or television programs
   - interviews

   Always assess the validity (Is it true? Is the research recent?) and credibility (Who are the authors? Why are they saying this?) of your sources.

3. Make point-form notes based on what you find. Make your notes detailed and focused on your topic. Do not copy the information word for word from your sources. Summarize it. You can avoid copying by studying the material carefully and then taking notes without looking at the source. Paraphrasing, or restating the information in your own words, helps you to understand what you are reading.

Skills *for* Social *Action*

4. Look carefully at your notes and decide on headings for your paragraphs. You should have an introductory paragraph, a concluding one, and a number of paragraphs in the middle. The way paragraphs are organized for a report depends on the topic you choose.

5. Organize your notes into the same categories as your paragraph headings. You must decide which information to leave out and which to include. You may also have to go back and find out more information for a particular paragraph.

6. Write the paragraphs. When writing paragraphs, begin each one with a clear topic sentence that explains what the paragraph will be about. Other sentences in the paragraph should support the topic sentence. The paragraph should end with a concluding statement or a sentence that links the paragraph to the one that follows.

7. Revise and edit your report. When revising, check to make sure the content is accurate, that the writing makes sense, and that you have used appropriate vocabulary. When editing, check for omissions and errors in spelling, punctuation, and grammar.

8. Present your report in an appropriate format. Your teacher may give you a specific format in which to present your report. If so, follow it carefully. If you are able to choose your own format, select one that is effective for the topic you have chosen.

Unit Conclusion

1. Create a visual metaphor for your ideal world. Use pictures and symbols to represent your main ideas. Explain how your visual metaphor reveals your personal beliefs and values, and do research into key areas of democratic citizenship.

2. Develop and present an evidence-based and persuasive public service announcement about world hunger, the exploitation of children, or how to become a globally minded consumer.

3. Locate two articles in the media—one concerning a human rights violation in Canada, and the other about a human rights violation in another nation. Analyze the response of both citizens and governments to these issues. Suggest your own solutions and effective ways to take action. Summarize and report your findings. Refer to Skills for Social Action on pages 198–200 to help you in your analysis.

4. Research and create a timeline that identifies a total of 10 significant dates, events, people, and struggles that record the development of the human rights of people with disabilities in Canada. Create a petition that advocates increased recognition of the rights of people with disabilities.

5. Create a "Tribute to Peace" dramatic minute based on the actions of a person or organization that you research. Refer to Skills for Social Action on pages 198–200 to help you in your research process.

6. Create 10 survey questions to ask your peers to identify their level of environmental citizenship.

7. Present a newscast that illustrates the struggle for cultural identity, economic independence, and human rights of an indigenous people of your choice. Write a paragraph that shows your research and comments on how the UN declaration, if followed by all nations worldwide, would benefit the indigenous peoples whom you studied.

Unit Conclusion

8. Create an advertising poster for the UN highlighting its achievements.

9. Research a genocide. Find information on the background to the event, the causes and conditions, the events of the genocide, and world reaction. Educate other people on your findings. Refer to Skills for Social Action on pages 198–200 to help you in your research process.

10. Write a letter as a student of the future. In the letter, dated 2085, you will reveal the state of the global village economically, politically, culturally, and technologically.

Reading to Learn

Here are a variety of strategies to help you read this textbook. Some strategies will help you before you start to read, others as you read, and others after you read. Choose the strategies that help you to understand and discuss the reading selection the most.

To be a good reader, it is important to **plan ahead.** Before you start to read, make sure you know what is expected of you after reading the selection. In this way, you can decide which strategies you need to complete the after-reading assignment. Remember: **If you don't know why you're reading, you won't know what to look for as you read.**

BEFORE READING

Before you begin to read, **skim and preview** the textbook to get a general idea of the content.

- Read the titles of the units, the headings, and subheadings.
- Look at the photos and other visuals, and check for clues on the pages.
- Do you have a general idea of what the content of the textbook will be?

Before you begin to read a unit or a section, do the same thing.

- Read the title of the unit, the heading, and the subheadings.
- Look at the photos and search for clues on the pages to give you a general idea of the content.
- Consider what you already know about the topic.

- Have you read something about this topic in another class?
- Have you seen information about it on television?
- Do members of your family talk about it sometimes?

You can use this **prior knowledge** to **make connections** between what you already know and what you are about to learn.

You might decide to create a web or a list to make connections between what you already know and what you would like to know about the topic. For example, you already know what an argument is, but you might like to know how to resolve conflict in your school. Since Unit 1: The Good Citizen, addresses this topic, if you think about what you know ahead of time, you will be better prepared to think about a response when you begin to read.

Before you begin to read a unit or a section, **ask yourself questions** to consider what you want to find out. **Hint:** Write your questions on a sheet of paper, and answer them as you read. Thinking about the question words—Who? What? Where? When? Why? How?—before you read helps you organize your thoughts and guide your reading.

DURING READING

As you read, think about what you need to know.

- If you **asked yourself questions** before you started, look for the answers as you read.

- Once you have found the answers, write them down next to the questions in point form.

- Later on, you can transfer the answers to a graphic organizer or a paragraph, or whatever makes sense to you and helps you understand.

As you read, **take notes.** This helps you identify the **main ideas.** In a **graphic organizer,** you can include the main ideas and any supporting details you think are important to remember. Textbooks usually contain clues to help you identify the main ideas: look for definitions in the margins or bold or coloured text. Questions such as those found in the "Let's Discuss" notes in the margins are designed to help you focus on main ideas.

If you find it difficult to understand the content of a reading selection, **pause and think** about it.

- Ask yourself what it is that you do not understand and what you need to figure out.

- Go back over your questions and answers, and your notes.

- When you are ready, **reread** the selection.

- Put the information down in your own words so that you understand it.

Sometimes, you may encounter words with meanings you don't know. When this happens, **think of a word that looks similar,** such as a word that has the same root. You might also reread the text, paying attention to how the word is used **in context.** Think about whether or not you have seen the word before, and **sound it out** if you find that this helps you understand.

As you read, close your eyes and **picture the situation** you are reading about. Think about your own experiences.

- Have you ever seen a situation like this one?

- Have you ever heard people talking about something similar?

- Could you **sketch** the scene?

Using your imagination and personal experiences can help you understand the context of a selection.

When you have finished reading the selection, take a few minutes to **summarize** what you have read. This is an important step since it helps you record the content in your own words. There are many ways to summarize.

- You can put relevant information in a chart so you can see it at a glance.

- You can highlight information in point-form notes.

- You can sketch a scene depicting relevant information.

- You can write a précis in paragraph-form.

Remember these are your notes; you should create them in such a way that you can understand and remember them.

AFTER READING

Once you have read the selection, you should take a few moments to **think about what you have read.**

- Decide if you need to reread portions of the selection.

- Make sure you understand the important words in context.

- Make sure you have noted the main ideas and some supporting details.

- Ask yourself if you understand enough to be able to discuss the topic, form an opinion, and justify your conclusions.

An integral part of reading for information is **drawing conclusions** and **forming opinions.** The "Let's Discuss" notes in the margins are designed to help you focus on these strategies. Once you have completed the selection, read the questions and think about how you would answer them. By doing so immediately after reading, you will be ready to express your opinions when it comes time to discuss the topic in your groups.

Remember: When reading for information, use all the strategies available to you to help you understand the topic, remember what you read, draw conclusions, and justify your opinions. Not all students will use the same strategies, nor will you use the same strategies each time you read. Choosing the strategies that best suit you, however, will make it easier for you to learn and to apply what you have learned.

Learning How to Learn

On the following pages, you will find a variety of ideas to help you understand content and complete assignments.

See also the **Skills for Social Action** features for the following strategies:

ANALYZING

Analyzing means separating a whole into parts or components in order to understand it.

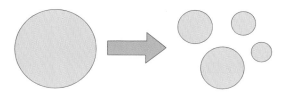

Reading Tip

Using a graphic organizer can help you analyze the information in a selection.

BRAINSTORMING

Brainstorming is a strategy for coming up with as many ideas about a topic as possible, and then choosing the best ones.

Suggestions for Brainstorming

1. Write down all ideas. Do not evaluate or criticize ideas as they are mentioned.

2. Quickly add ideas to the list. Don't reflect whether the idea is "good" or not. Unusual ideas should be included in your list.

3. Sometimes thinking about one idea leads to another. Add to, subtract from, join, and change ideas to come up with new ones. The more ideas you have, the better.

4. Reflect about your ideas and choose the best ones.

CAUSE AND EFFECT (RESULT)

A cause is something that makes an event or situation occur. The event or situation then leads to an effect (result).

- Use a diagram to help you understand cause-and-effect ideas.

- The words "reasons for" and "consequences" signal cause and effect.

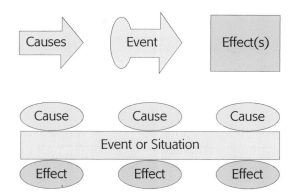

Reading Tip

If you are having difficulty understanding the cause-and-effect relationship described in a selection, think about the relationship in terms of a problem and a solution. Remember, however, that events often have many causes and many effects.

CHARTS AND GRAPHIC ORGANIZERS

Charts are ways to organize, record, and display information. You can use them to help you make notes. Charts are also referred to as diagrams, tables, or graphs.

Retrieval Chart

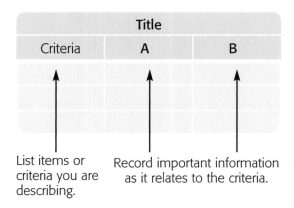

Flow Chart

Flow charts are diagrams of ideas in sequence (order). Flow charts can show classification, relationships, possibilities, or choices.

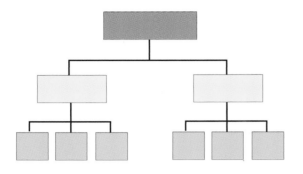

Webs and Mind Maps

Write the title in the centre and notes in the "doughnut pieces," one idea per piece. Add to or take away partitions from the doughnut as needed.

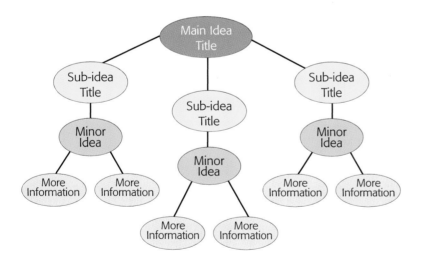

Mind maps work much like webs. Each idea is placed on a separate line. Each word or idea must be joined by a line to at least one other word or idea.

CLASSIFYING

To classify, you gather together ideas, events, or items and arrange them into groups that have common characteristics. Each of us thinks differently, so there are many ways to classify information. A flow chart is one way to do this.

Steps for Classifying

1. List items or examples randomly.
2. Identify and label groups (categories) based on their characteristics.
3. Sort into groups based on similarities.
4. (Optional) Record information on a graphic organizer, such as a flow chart.

COMPARING

This thinking tool is used to show how something is similar to, and different from, something else.

Words Used in Making Comparisons

- although
- as well as
- but
- also
- either
- however
- like

- not only
- on the other hand
- or
- similarly
- unless
- unlike
- yet

Comparison Chart

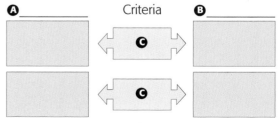

Steps for Comparing

1. Identify what you are comparing.

2. Identify what criteria you are going to use in comparing. The number of criteria will vary depending upon what you are comparing. Record in the middle column of the Comparison Chart.

3. Show how the items you are comparing are the same (or how they are different), based on the criteria you identified.

Venn Diagram

The Venn diagram is used for comparison.

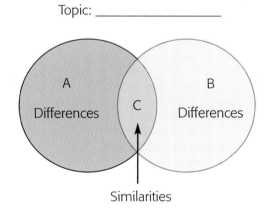

Topic: _____

Reading Tip

After reading a difficult selection, creating a chart or diagram for that selection can help you clarify, interpret, and analyze the information.

CONCEPT POSTER

A concept poster is an information display that is more than just visual. Concept posters are a fun way to learn, remember new information, and share what you've learned with your classmates. They may be done individually, in pairs, or as a small group.

Steps for Concept Posters

Step 1:

a) Review information about the concept in your textbook and your notebook.

b) List examples.

c) Brainstorm to decide what the examples have in common. Look for patterns, links, and connections.

Step 2: Plan and create a presentation to represent your ideas and examples about the concept. You could include any of the following:

- picture (photo, drawing, map, or diagram)
- skit or tableau
- music/song/sound effects
- words (spoken or on paper)
- objects/models

Step 3: Present your concept poster to your classmates. You may either tell them what concept you are presenting or have them guess.

TIMELINE

A timeline is a way to show events chronologically. It can include words, numerals, and pictures.

How to Read a Timeline

- Timelines can be horizontal (across) or vertical (up and down).
- If a timeline is in scale, the years will be marked evenly along the line. If a timeline is not in scale, the specific dates are in sequence but not arranged in proportion. This usually occurs when some events shown were very far apart and others very close together in time.

Reading Tip

When reading about events, pay particular attention to any references to dates and to words such as *before, after, then, meanwhile, finally.* Sometimes the events may not be related in a straightforward manner (chronological order). As you read, try to organize the events in your head. After reading, create a timeline or flow chart to show the correct sequence of events. It may also be helpful to think of the cause-and-effect relationships surrounding events.

CARTOON ANALYSIS

Cartoons are drawings in which the artist exaggerates features to make a statement of opinion about the subject of the cartoon. (Cartoons appeal to the reader's emotions.)

- The purpose of a political cartoon is to get readers to look closely at the subject, question their views on it, and sometimes change their opinion about it.

- Political cartoons portray public figures, the general public, institutions (such as the government), and news events.

- Many cartoons use humour for a serious purpose (not just to be funny).

- Some of the information in cartoons is factual, and some information is symbolic. The reader's goal is to interpret the information shown and understand the cartoonist's message about the subject.

Steps for Interpreting Political Cartoons

Step 1: Examine what you see. Every detail has been included for a reason.

- the setting (public buildings, locations)

- the news story to which it relates

- the character(s): Who does the character represent? (A character may stand for the general public, a member of a specific group, or a well-known person.)

- symbols, such as flags, logos, animals, or objects that represent something else (for example, the beaver is a symbol for Canada)

Step 2: Analyze what you see.

- What looks important or powerful? The foreground and the centre are important positions in a picture. The important parts of a picture are large, stand out, have more detail, or attract your attention in some way.

- What looks powerless? (may be small, in a low position, at the back, portrayed as weak)

- How does the cartoon make you feel? How do the characters make you feel?

- Stereotypes are often used to identify a character as belonging to a certain group. They may show negative bias.

- Caricature of facial features may be used to identify public figures.

- Words in cartoons give important information.

- When and where was the cartoon published? The common opinions and attitudes toward issues in the historical period can help you understand the intended message of the cartoon.

Step 3: Examine the cartoonist's attitude and purpose.

- Does the cartoonist praise or criticize the different characters or the event?

- Is something being made fun of? being explained? being revealed (made public)?
- Is a certain point of view given?
- Is something being distorted or made ugly or frightening?

CRITICAL THINKING

Critical thinking means not accepting information just as it is presented to you, but questioning it to confirm its accuracy.

Facts and Opinion

The information that you receive was chosen by someone and gives that person's point of view. Facts may be accurate or they may be wrong or confused. They involve the writer or speaker's opinion about facts. It is important to be able to distinguish between factual information and opinion.

- A fact is something that is supported by evidence and is not contradicted by other evidence. It can be checked, and most people agree about it.
- An opinion is something believed to be so. Opinion may be based on fact. However, unless evidence is given to confirm or prove it, you must question it.

Example

Sir John A. Macdonald was Canada's first prime minister. (fact)

Sir John A. Macdonald was Canada's most important prime minister. (opinion)

Bias

Learning to detect bias is an important part of critical thinking. Bias means showing a preference by portraying something positively or negatively. Bias shows the author/artist's opinion about the subject. Bias can distort the facts, so it is important to recognize when it occurs.

Examine images and text carefully.

- Do the photographs or illustrations portray the subject negatively or positively?
- What words are used? Are they negative or positive?
- What facts are given, and what facts are left out?
- Are people, ideas, places, or events distorted in order to criticize or make fun of them?
- How do you think you were intended to feel about the subject?

Reading Tip — Bias

As you read, think about what the author says, but also consider what the author does not say. An important part of identifying bias is noting which points of view are not addressed, and which facts are ignored or overlooked. Think also about the original audience and purpose for the passage. This knowledge will give you clues to the author's bias.

A Critical Thinking Model

Step 1: Identify the issue, and examine the information you already have about this issue.

- Are your facts accurate?
- Are there any ideas that do not relate or work together or ideas that contradict one another?
- How reliable is the information?

Step 2: Identify the various people who will have different points of view in a situation.

- Who are the various people who would have an interest in, and opinion about, this issue?

Step 3: Try "stepping out" of your own point of view and thinking about what one or more of the other people might think about this issue.

- Why does a person think the way he or she does?

- Why does a person think his or her way is best?

- Why does she or he choose to do things differently?

- What might a person be feeling to act the way he or she does?

- What might a person be thinking to have certain feelings?

DEBATES

Debates may be formal or informal, but they always have some rules. A debate has a purpose, a structure, and a conclusion.

Purpose

A debate is an organized way to discuss and come to a conclusion about an issue. The issue is stated at the beginning. All of the discussion must relate to it. Discussion may have two sides (as in a formal debate) or many different sides (as in a round-table debate with a chairperson).

Structure

In a debate, one person at a time speaks and the other participants listen. Either there is a particular order in which participants speak, or someone acts as chairperson. In a chaired debate, speakers signal and are given permission to speak.

Conclusion

The last speakers in the debate sum up the discussion for their sides. There is more than one way to come to a conclusion on the issue. In a formal debate, a moderator may judge the points that have been made by each side and decide which side made the best arguments. In a round-table debate, there may be a vote.

Reading Tip

As you conduct research to prepare for a formal debate, organize your notes into two columns.

Facts Supporting Your Point of View	Facts Supporting Your Opponent's Point of View

INTERPRETING IMAGES

Photographs, paintings, illustrations, and drawings are excellent sources of information. You should "read" visuals for information as you would read words.

In your mind, divide the photograph into parts. Look for details, then ask yourself the first set of questions. Not all questions will apply to all photographs.

Make a quick web or point-form notes answering these five questions:

1. What do you see in this picture? Describe details in each part of the photo.

2. Who is in the photo? What are the people doing? What is happening?

3. Where do you think this picture was taken?

4. When? How can you tell?

5. Why do you think the photograph was taken or the picture drawn?

Other questions and activities

1. How are people dressed? What does this tell about them?

2. Notice their facial expressions. What feelings do you think the people are expressing?

3. How do people seem to be relating to, or interacting with, each other?

4. Put yourself in the place of one of the people in the photo. How would you feel?

5. Locate buildings. Describe them. Are they old or new? Are they for living in or for work? What type of technology was used to build them?

6. Examine transportation and communication methods.

7. Examine the level of technology.

8. Examine the geographic features: landforms, climate, vegetation, rivers, and other bodies of water. How do these features affect human activity?

Reading Tip

Make connections between the visual and the text around it. Ask yourself: Why was this visual included? How does it support the text? How does it contradict the text? What other visual would I have found to be more useful?

DECISION MAKING

Decision-making is a process used to resolve an issue. Issues are problems or questions for debate. They are often written as a question using the word "should." For example, Should students be allowed to wear whatever they like to school?

There is often not a definite answer to an issue. A person must choose from several alternatives. As a result, opinions and emotions are often involved.

A Decision Making Model

Step 1: Decide: What is the issue to be solved?

Step 2: Brainstorm for alternatives (choices).

Step 3: Analyze the alternatives. List the consequences (results) of each. That is, list the pros (+) and the cons (−).

Step 4: Decide what options are best. Try to select the alternative(s) with the most positive and the fewest negative consequences. Organize the alternatives in rank order, from the most desirable to the least desirable.

Step 5: What is your decision? Choose the "best" alternative.

Step 6: Evaluate your results. Ask yourself these questions:

- Was this a fair and effective decision? Why?

- What difficulties are expected from this decision?

- What benefits are expected from this decision?

- Faced with the same issue again, would I change my decision? Why?

- What changes or improvements might be made to this method of decision making?

Decision Making Chart

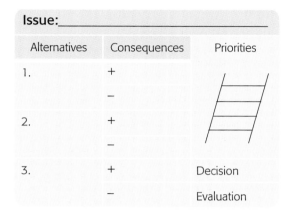

ESSAY WRITING

An essay is a written composition on a certain subject. The purpose of an essay is to demonstrate that you understand a topic or to persuade a reader to share your point of view. An essay assignment often takes the form of a question beginning with "Why," "Should," or "To what extent." An essay can also be called a position paper.

Before Writing

- Read the topic or question carefully. (You cannot demonstrate your understanding if you don't understand the question.)

- Brainstorm ideas about a possible thesis, arguments, and supporting evidence.

- Make quick notes of ideas that occur to you. Use a web to show how ideas relate to each other.

A **thesis** is a statement that is made about a topic and defended with evidence and logical argument.

Argument is reasons that show your thesis is correct and the opposite point of view is wrong.

Constructing an Essay

Regardless of length, an essay should include an introduction, a body, and a conclusion.

Introduction

To demonstrate understanding, you will need to introduce the topic. Write an overview about what your essay includes or the problem to be examined. Make a statement that answers the assigned question. This is your thesis.

Your thesis provides the focus of the essay and limits what you will write about. Recall your thesis regularly while writing your essay. It will help you

- avoid answering a different question than you started out to answer

- avoid adding extra details that don't support your argument (your thesis)

Body

Your essay needs to be well organized and persuasive.

- Take the ideas and supporting evidence you came up with initially and begin to organize them. Use charts and graphic organizers to organize your ideas, or make an outline of the order in which you will present your arguments and evidence.

- The length of an essay can vary. However, even in a short essay, you should support your thesis with a minimum of three important ideas. Present your arguments and evidence logically to support your thesis.

- The simplest way is to present each argument as the topic sentence of a paragraph. Then support each argument with evidence in the same paragraph. Each point you make should lead to the next. All of the points should relate to the topic sentence. Do not include information that does not belong.

- Each paragraph in the body should also lead logically to the next. Use transition words and phrases to link ideas in your argument logically.

Examples of Transition Words

- with this in mind
- then
- as a result
- therefore
- later
- as well
- in a similar way
- however
- on the other hand
- so
- furthermore

Conclusion

Sum up your arguments by restating them. If possible, link them together in your final statement in order to persuade your reader that you are right about your thesis.

Reading Tip

Before writing an essay, further research may be required. Take notes to summarize information that you are researching. Remember to provide footnotes and a bibliography for any text that is not your own.

GRAPHS

Graphs are used to present numerical information visually.

Bar Graphs

- used for comparison; may compare range in one or more items; for example, time, distance, quantity

- the vertical scale (y-axis) is marked in regular intervals (e.g., intervals of 10 percent) measuring the items being compared

- the unit of measurement is stated on the y-axis and the regular intervals shown

- the bottoms of the bars are placed on the horizontal base (x–axis)

- the bars are named or a colour-key used to identify them

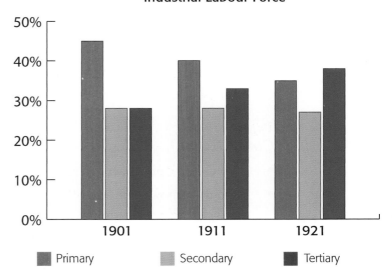

Industrial Labour Force

■ Primary   ■ Secondary   ■ Tertiary

Line Graphs

- used to show trends over time
- the vertical (y-axis) line is marked at regular intervals; it shows changes that occur (e.g., intervals of $25 000 million)
- the horizontal (x-axis) line is marked in regular intervals; it is almost always labelled with units of time (e.g., yearly intervals)
- the unit of measurement on each axis is stated and the regular intervals shown

Industrial Production in Canada

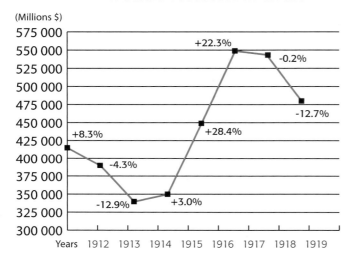

Ontario

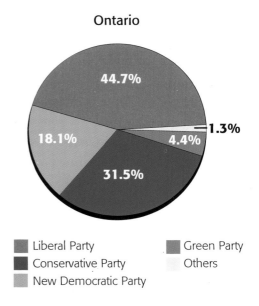

Liberal Party
Conservative Party
New Democratic Party
Green Party
Others

Reading Tip

Some learners find it easier to understand information presented in a graph, while others find it easier to understand information presented in text. Whichever type of learner you are, use both the graph and the text to support your understanding of the information.

NOTE MAKING

T-Notes

T-Notes combine written notes and drawings. Use the format below, or design your own.

Main title
• Write one or two sentences to describe what this section is about.

Drawing or sketch	Sub-titles
	• Write notes in point form here.

Circle Graphs

- also called "pie charts"
- used to compare the size of a part (or parts) to the whole amount or number
- usually created using percentages or fractions: the sum of the parts must equal 100 percent of something (e.g., population of a region)

Point-Form Notes (Rough Notes)

Writing point-form notes involves reading a section, thinking about the main or most important ideas, and recording these ideas in your own words (paraphrasing). Your goal is to record only the most important ideas, using your own words.

Some ideas

- Use chapter and section headings.
- Under each heading, record only key words/ideas.
- Do not write in complete sentences. Use a dash (–) to begin new ideas.
- Use abbreviations.

Reading Tip

In order to make effective notes, you will need to identify the main idea and the most important supporting details in the text. The Focus Questions and section headings will help you to identify the main ideas in the text.

NOTEBOOK ORGANIZATION

Your notebook is your record of the material you have studied. Your notes need to be easy to use and study from.

Organization Suggestions

- Keep notes in sequence. Either date them and make them chronological, or sort and organize them by topic using dividers in a binder.
- Create a table of contents for each section and chapter.
- Keep the pages in order. Add new information to the back of your old notes.

- Compare your notebook with that of a partner to check for items that are missing or out of order.
- Use colours to underline, highlight, illustrate, and code your notes. Colours help us to learn material.
- When you study, use the margins to add diagrams, list key words, write out definitions, refer to other sections of your notes, or connect to page numbers from the textbook.
- Develop a vocabulary of terms and unfamiliar words.

STUDY SKILLS

It is important to have good study skills and use them regularly. Study skills will help you learn new material, review, and prepare for exams.

Methods of Studying

- Learn by teaching a friend or parent.
- Team study. Question each other. Read each other's notes—someone else's way of expressing an idea may stick with you. Get them to explain notes you do not understand. This will help both of you.
- Use interviewing and role-playing to understand and be able to explain the point of view of important people. You may need to write an assignment from someone's point of view.
- Use practice tests. Review old exams, predict the types of questions you may face, and practise sample answers.

Test Questions

Make up your own exam questions, and share them with others. For example, make the chapter headings into questions.

Use the chapter headings to make up questions that ask the following:

- who
- why
- where
- contrast
- cause/effect
- when
- what
- compare
- describe
- classify

PRESENTATIONS

In this book, presentation refers to communicating information in visual, oral, or written forms. To prepare and carry out a presentation, follow these steps:

Step 1: First, select one main topic or idea as a focus for your presentation. Everything you do must be related to, or provide examples of, this main idea.

Step 2: Select a method of presentation from the list that follows. Find out from your teacher or the library how you are to make or prepare it if you do not know.

Step 3: Read about your topic or idea in the textbook. Review any information you have about it in your research notes.

Step 4: Plan on paper how you are going to prepare the presentation you selected. Establish criteria for how to assess your presentation.

Step 5: Prepare the presentation on the topic or idea you selected.

Step 6: Present your topic or idea to your classmates. Assess your presentation based on the criteria from Step 4.

Some Presentation Ideas

advertisement

cartoon

collage

debate

diagram

display

map

multimedia presentation

mural

newspaper article

oral report

panel discussion

poster

radio show

role-play/drama

speech

talk show

PROBLEM SOLVING

A problem is a difficult question that requires you to consider a number of possible solutions in order to choose the best. For certain kinds of problems (e.g., a math problem), there is one correct answer. However, there are many problems in life that have more than one solution.

Problems ask: Who? What? Where?

When? Why? How?

Steps for Problem Solving

Step 1: Define the problem. Decide what you want to find out.

Step 2: Come up with possible questions and a hypothesis to guide your research.

(A hypothesis is a rough guess about the solution, based on what you know.)

Step 3: Do research to locate data (information) that relates to your hypothesis.

Step 4: Record the data (information) that relates to your hypothesis.

Step 5: Evaluate the information you have collected by thinking about whether it supports or disagrees with your hypothesis.

Step 6: Arrive at a conclusion by choosing what you think is the best solution—one that makes sense and solves the problem. Think about whether your conclusion agrees or disagrees with your hypothesis.

Step 7: Share your conclusion.

Problem-solving Chart

Problem	
Hypothesis	
Research Solution	Data
1.	
2.	
3.	
4.	
I think #_____ is the best solution because	

RESEARCHING USING THE INTERNET

The Internet is a network of computers around the world that are able to communicate with one another. When you go online to research a topic, it means your computer is connected to this World Wide Web (the Web) of computers. The World Wide Web is made up of Web sites.

Anyone can publish anything they want on the Internet. No one checks the information for accuracy. Web sites can contain false and inaccurate information. It is always a good idea to ask, "Who produced this information?" when collecting information on the Internet. Information posted on the Internet by a government agency or an institution, such as a university, is likely to be more accurate than information created by an individual.

Do Not Plagiarize

When you find useful information on the Internet, it is often tempting to just cut and copy sections from the Web site right into your own document. Copying other people's work without permission and calling it your own is called plagiarism. It is illegal. Record where information comes from, and put quotation marks around work you take directly from a Web site. Even if you use ideas from a Web site and write the information in your own words, you should record the online source you used.

Safe Surfing

When you are using the Internet, you need to be cautious about personal information you share. Never give out personal information (name, phone number, address, credit card numbers) over the Internet. Never agree to meet someone you have met online. If you want to subscribe to an Internet newsletter or register at a Web site, discuss this with your parents first. Have them check out the Web site.

Ad banners appear on nearly all of the commercial Web sites. They are the same as the advertisements you see on television. If you click on ad banners promising you prizes, free products, or chances to win money, you will be linked to a Web site that will try to sell you something. Never buy anything on the Internet until your parents have checked out the Web site.

Get your parents' or your teacher's permission before looking for information on the Internet. Use only search engines and Web sites they have seen and approved. Tell your parents and/or teacher about unusual behaviour or objectionable material you encounter online.

WRITING

There are many types of writing. The form in which you write could include any of those described briefly on these two pages, or others. Your purpose for writing might include telling, persuading, explaining, reporting, describing. Think about your purpose and your audience so you can choose the most effective form and words. Challenge yourself by writing in a variety of forms.

Persuading

Persuasive writing is intended to convince your reader to accept your point of view. Take care to use appropriate language and visuals. Hurting or insulting people will not change their viewpoints.

Persuading can be used in the following forms of writing:

Advertisement

- Announcement or written notice for the public

- Provides information that is meant to persuade people to act in a certain way (e.g., buy a product, vote for a candidate)
- Words and pictures should catch people's attention

Brochure/Pamphlet/Flyer

- Usually a small booklet or folded sheet providing details (written and visual) that highlight the most appealing features of a place, person, event, idea

Editorial

- An article (short essay) found in most newspapers that expresses an opinion on behalf of the newspaper about a current event or issue in the news
- Includes facts that support a point of view and strengthen an argument

Essay

- A written composition on a certain subject

Letter to the Editor

- Letter written to a newspaper to express opinions about current events or issues
- Includes facts that support a point of view and strengthen a position
- May contain emotional and descriptive words

Review or Critique

- An evaluation or judgement of a product or performance (e.g., play, movie, artwork, CD, book)
- Gives information that supports the writer's claims and opinions
- Can include emotional and descriptive words

Speech

- May serve many different purposes (e.g., entertaining, paying tribute, congratulating); often intended to persuade or convince (e.g., campaign speech)
- Intended to be spoken to an audience
- Words should be appropriate for the audience and the situation
- Planning and practising out loud are needed; volume, expression, pace, posture, and gestures give added meaning and impact to the words
- Point-form notes (cue cards) may be used when presenting but should not be read

Explaining

This type of writing helps the reader understand how to do something and how/why something works as it does.

Explaining can be used in the following forms of writing:

Instructions/Directions/Manual

- Provide a step-by-step order.
- Use clear language that is easy to follow.
- Use special terms that relate to the topic and suit the audience (e.g., "sifting" is a suitable term in a recipe).

Reporting

Reports use knowledge gathered from a variety of sources and provide factual information. Reporting can be used in the following forms of writing:

Census

- A specific count of the people living in an area

- Might include information about ages, jobs, education, and religion

News Report

- Describes a current event of importance to the readers
- Answers who, what, where, when, why, and how
- Factual; may include quotations from people expressing opinions

Magazine Feature Article

- Provides information about people, places, and events that are of interest to the readers
- Usually requires an interview or other research
- Includes visuals

Research Report

- Provides detailed information on a specific topic or issue
- Can be presented in a number of ways

Survey/Poll/Questionnaire

- An investigation about a situation or issue
- Includes clear, specific questions intended for a certain group
- Poll should allow for responses that are easily recorded and counted (e.g., Yes/No responses)
- Results may be presented in graphs, charts, tables, or paragraphs
- Polls should avoid bias; choose a large, random sample rather then just people you expect to answer a certain way

Glossary

A

Aboriginal peoples A collective term that refers to the three different groups of people—First Nations, Inuit, and Métis people in Canada; their ancestors were the indigenous or first peoples who inhabited North America.

advance poll The poll is the place you go to vote. Some of these polls are open before election day to allow citizens to vote in advance.

annexed To take over territory and make it part of another state.

arbitrary Chosen at random.

arbitration A third party is given the power to decide the outcome of the conflict.

assimilation The absorbing of a minority group into the majority.

autocracy A type of government in which one person (an autocrat) rules with absolute power.

autocratic decision making A process by which one person makes a decision for a group.

autonomy Personal independence or freedom.

B

basic needs Things people need for physical survival, such as food, shelter, and clothing.

bias Showing a preference by portraying something positively or negatively. It can distort facts.

bill A document that outlines a new law to be set before Parliament for consideration.

boycott An effort by a group to refuse to deal with a person or organization to protest its actions.

C

candidate A person who chooses to run in an election; often a person who has been chosen by a political party to run for office.

committee A group of the legislature that reviews proposed laws.

common good What will make the most people safe, secure, and happy.

conciliation A third party clearly defines both the points of agreement and the points of difference that must be resolved to end the conflict.

consensual/collaborative decision making A process by which everyone in the group must agree before a decision is made.

consensus A general agreement or opinion that is sought through discussion, not a vote.

consensus building A process by which a group makes a decision only when everyone is in agreement.

Constitution The body of rules or laws by which Canada is governed; passed in 1982, it contains Canada's new *Charter of Rights and Freedoms*, the amending formula, and the 1867 *British North America Act*.

D

democracy A type of government in which citizens elect their government, usually by electing representatives.

democratic decision making A process by which a group decision is made by a majority vote.

discrimination The unfavourable or prejudiced treatment of an individual or group based on race, sex, appearance, income, and so on.

diversity A variety of people, cultures, beliefs, and so on.

E

election A process by which citizens vote for their representatives in government from a list of candidates running for office.

electoral district A defined area where voters elect a member of a legislature. A riding.

F

First Nations Distinct nations of people sharing common ancestry such as Mi'kmaq, Dene, Mohawk, Cree, Ojibway, Siksika (Blackfoot); replaces the term *Indian*.

first past the post (FPTP) An electoral system in which the candidate receiving more votes than any other wins a seat in government.

franchise The right of citizens of a country, such as Canada, to vote in their country's elections. The federal franchise is related to voting in federal elections.

G

genocide The deliberate extermination of a group of people, especially one of a particular race, nation, or culture.

H

Holocaust The mass murder of Jews and other "undesirables" by the Nazis during World War II.

human dignity The feeling that one is respected and valued in a society.

human rights Basic rights and freedoms to which all citizens are entitled.

I

impartial Fair and free of bias.

inequalities A term often used to refer to the differences in our society where some people have more money, education, and other resources than other people; these differences may be the result of discrimination.

inequitable Unequal, unfair.

interconnected Connected with each other.

interdependent Dependent on each other.

interest group A group of people that represents a particular occupation or common goal and influences governments to pass laws favouring these goals.

Inuit Aboriginal people who live in Arctic Canada, Northern Quebec, and Labrador.

L

legislation The act or process of making laws; also the laws made.

legislature A body of people with the power to make laws.

lobbyist A registered representative of a company or interest group who tries to influence government policy.

M

majority Most people; an election in which one candidate receives more than 50 percent of the total number of votes.

mediation A third party helps both parties arrive at a solution to the conflict.

Métis Aboriginal people whose ancestors were of mixed heritage (First Nations or Inuit, and European) and whose culture is distinctly Métis.

multicultural A description of a nation, such as Canada, that allows many different ethnic groups to retain their own languages, religions, and cultures with tolerance and without discrimination.

multinational corporations Large business organizations based in one country that have multiple factories and offices in other countries.

N

negotiation Both parties discuss the issues and try to resolve differences, being careful to avoid negative, blaming language. Usually both parties have to give up some of their demands in order to reach a compromise.

nomination The process by which a person is selected to run for elected office.

non-government organization (NGO) An organization that is not part of any government; NGOs are often non-profit citizens' groups with specific goals in mind.

non-status Indians First Nation people who are not registered as Indians under the *Indian Act*. Their ancestors gave up their Indian status to be able to vote and were removed from a list of status Indians, or they were not originally registered after treaties were signed with the government of Canada.

non-treaty Indians First Nation people whose ancestors did not sign treaties with the British or Canadian government, either before or after Confederation in 1867.

P

peacekeeping The overseeing of a halt in fighting between nations or groups; Canadian Lester Pearson won the Nobel Peace Prize for "inventing" modern peacekeeping.

petition A formal written request signed by many people.

plurality The election result where one candidate receives more votes than any other, but less than 50 percent of the total votes.

political ideology The system of ideas or beliefs about government that guides a person or political party.

political parties Organized groups with similar ideas about government and politics who run candidates for office and who seek to form a government.

political socialization The way we learn our political beliefs.

popular vote The total number of votes cast by voters in an election.

power The ability of an individual or group to get what it wants.

proportional representation (PR) An electoral system that distributes seats according to the percentage of the total votes received by each party.

psychological needs Things people need for emotional reasons, such as safety and security.

R

ratified To approve or confirm formally.

reenfranchised To get back the right to vote (franchise).

referendum A process that allows every citizen a say on some question of importance to a nation or community by means of a direct vote.

riding A defined area where voters elect a member of a legislature. An electoral district or constituency.

Royal Commission A government-appointed group of citizens responsible for investigating in detail and making recommendations about an issue of national or provincial concern.

S

separatists Individuals who support the separation of a province from the nation; in Canada, there has been a separatist movement in Quebec since the 1960s.

society A community of people who share basic needs and wants.

sovereignty Independence or nationhood; in Canada, Aboriginal or Quebec sovereignty is a goal shared by some, but not all, residents of Canada.

Speech from the Throne A statement of the legislative program or bills that a provincial or federal government intends to pass in the coming session of Parliament. The speech is delivered by the lieutenant governor or governor general to the assembled legislature.

status Indians People who are registered under the *Indian Act* as members of a particular First Nation. They have the right to live on a specific Indian reserve but may choose to live off the reserve and still retain status.

sustainability Using resources, such as water and forests, in such a way that they are not used up or damaged.

T

treaty Indians First Nations people whose ancestors signed treaties with the British or Canadian government, either before or after Confederation in 1867.

V

vigil A solemn meditation, prayer, or talk by a group of people, usually at night.

W

wants Goods or services that people desire but that are not necessary for survival.

Index

Visual Credits

Every reasonable effort has been made to trace the ownership of copyright material used in the text. The publisher would be pleased to know of any errors or omissions.

Front Cover: © Corel (O Canada!)

2–3 Ken Chernus/Taxi/Getty Images; 5 Comstock; 6 © 2005 Jupiter Images Corporation (Picture Quest/Ingram Publishing); 9 © Jeff Greenberg/Photo Edit Inc.; 10 Darren McCollester/Getty Images News; 11 collage clockwise from top left: CP/Aaron Harris, © David Young-Wolff/Photo Edit Inc., SW Productions/Brand X Images/Getty Images, © Reuters/Corbis; 13 © David Young-Wolff/Photo Edit Inc., 14 © Dave G. Houser/Corbis; 16 © Myrleen Ferguson Cate/Photo Edit Inc.; 17 © Joel W. Rogers/Corbis; 18 CP/Tom Hanson; 20: top © Ted Horowitz/Corbis, bottom Neo Vision/Photonica/Getty Images; 21 © 2005 Jupiter Images Corporation (Photos.com); 22 Eyewire Images (now Photodisc); 23 © Michael Newman/ Photo Edit Inc.; 24 Jim Young/Reuters/Landov; 27 © Gabe Palmer/Corbis; 28 Citizenship and Immigration Canada; 29 © Dave G. Houser/Corbis; 30 Halifax Port Authority Collection of the Pier 21 Society/Pier 21 Society; 31 Ron Bull/Toronto Star; 33 Stan Honda/AFP/Getty Images; 34 Penelope Breese/Getty Images; 35 Rick Madonik/Toronto Star/ First Light; 36 Photo of Etobicoke candidates Laurel Broten and Donna Cansfield in front of Donna Cansfield's campaign headquarters, 2003: permission courtesy of Donna Cansfield; 37 Elections Canada; 38 © Hulton-Deutsch Collection/Corbis; 39 CP/Frank Gunn; 41 Elections Canada; 42 Cyril Jessop/Library and Archives Canada/PA-030212; 43 copyleft by Wikipedia (http://en.wikipedia.org/wiki/ Ontario_general_election_2003); 44 © Bob Daemmrich/Photo Edit Inc.; 46 W.J. Moore/Library and Archives Canada/C-021594; 47 Victor Last/Geographical Visual Aids; 48 Jim Cochrane/First Light; 49: top © Corbis/Corbis, middle Chris Wattie/Reuters/ Landov; 54 CP/J.P. Moczulski; 55 Parks Canada/W. Waterton/06.64.09.11(04); 58 Donald Weber/Getty Images; 59 © Ed Bock/Corbis; 60 Shaun Best/Reuters/Landov; 64 Hothouse Canada; 65 © Shaun Best/Reuters/Corbis; 66 Jim Young/Reuters/Landov; 67 Ron Bull/Toronto Star; 70 David Cooper/Toronto Star; 71 © 2005 Jupiter Images Corporation (Photos.com); 72 CP/Ryan Remiorz; 73 © Davis Barber/Photo Edit Inc.; 74–75 Southern Ontario Model United Nations Association (SOMA) 2005; 76 Permission granted courtesy of The University of Western Ontario; 77 © Jeff Greenberg/Photo Edit Inc.; 78–79 CP/Ryan Remiorz; 81 copyleft by Wikipedia (http://en.wikipedia.org/wiki/ Human_Development_Index); 82 © Jonathan Nourok/ Photo Edit Inc.; 83 © Andrew Wallace/Reuters/Corbis; 84 © International Institute for Democracy and Electoral Assistance (IDEA)/ www.idea.int; 85 "Reasons For Not Voting" adapted from the following source: Elections Canada, Explaining the Turnout Decline in Canadian Federal Elections: A New Survey of Non-voters, March 2003, p. 17. Adaptation rests with the author; 86 "Age and Voting Turnout" adapted from the following source: Elections Canada, Explaining the Turnout Decline in Canadian Federal Elections: A New Survey of Non-voters, March 2003, p. 20. Adaptation rests with the author; 86 photograph © Michael Newman/Photo Edit Inc.;

88 © Toronto Star 2001; 89 © Toronto Star 2001; 90 AP/Al Grillo; 91 AP/Mario Suriani; 92 © Alan Schein Photography/ Corbis; 93 © 2005 Jupiter Images Corporation (ShutterStock); 94 Victor Last/Geographical Visual Aids; 95 Permission courtesy of Maude Barlow and the Council of Canadians; 96 © 2005 Jupiter Images Corporation (ShutterStock); 97 © Brooks Kraft/Corbis; 98 © Tony Freeman/ Photo Edit Inc./ 100 © Jim Young/Reuters/Corbis; 101 CP/Frank Gunn; 102 © Toronto Star 2001; 103 © Brooks Kraft/Corbis; 104 AFT/Hulton Archive/Getty Images; 105 Duncan Cameron/Library and Archives Canada/PA-C-25003; 106: left CP/Peter Bregg, centre © Bettman/Corbis; 107: top Victor Last/Geographical Visual Aids, centre © 1980 Bernard Brault/Klixpix/First Light; 108 CP/Ron Poling; 109 Bill Lowry/Ivy Images; 110 CP/John Ulan; 111: centre CP/Kevin Frayer, bottom Robesus Royalty Free Digital Images; 112 Bill Lowry/Ivy Images; 113 © Statistics Canada; 114 Permission courtesy of the Inuit Tapirisat Kenatami (ITK); 115 J. De Visser/Ivy Images; 116 Victor Last/Geographical Visual Aids; 117 © Michelle Meawasige: By permission of Michelle Meawasige and JoAnn Kakekayash; 119 Glenbow Archives NA-2864-27196; 120 © Christopher J. Morris/Corbis; 121 O. Bierwagen/ Ivy Images; 122 Bill Ivy/Ivy Images; 123 CP/Ryan Remiorz; 124 CP/Winnipeg Free Press/Wayne Glowacki; 125 CP/Fred Chartrand; 126 CP/Winnipeg Free Press/Ken Gigliotti; 127 CP/Paul Chiasson; 128 © David Young-Wolff/Photo Edit Inc.; 129 © 2005 Jupiter Images Corporation (ShutterStock); 130 © Spencer Grant/Photo Edit Inc.; 131 Robert E. Daemmrich/Stone/Getty Images; 132 © 2005 Jupiter Images Corporation (ShutterStock); 133 © David Young-Wolff/Photo Edit Inc.; 134–135 Reuters/DND/Landov; 137: top © Tony Gentile/Reuters/Corbis, bottom © Auslöser/Zefa/Forbis; 139 Al Harvey/www.slidefarm.com; 141 GDT/Stone/Getty Images; 142: top Corbis © Mike Theiss/Jim Reed Photography/Corbis, bottom © Neville Elder/Corbis; 143 Chip Simons/Getty Images; 144 HotHouse Canada; 145: top Colin McConnell/Toronto Star/ First Light, bottom © Denis Balibouse/Reuters/Corbis; 146: top HotHouse Canada, bottom © Joel Stettenheim/ Corbis; 147 AP/Stephen Chernin; 148 EPA/Narendra Shrestha/Landov; 149: centre © Sophie Elbaz/Sygma/Corbis, right © Ariel Skelley/Corbis; 150 © Patrick Robert/Sygma/Corbis; 151 Courtesy of Reebok Human Rights Foundation; 152 CP/Tom Hanson; 153 Antonio Mo/Taxi/Getty Images; 154 AP/Ben Margot; 155 Arif Ali/AFP/Getty Images; 156 © Jonathan Hayward/Pool/Reuters/Corbis; 157 Jean-Pierre Muller/AFT/Getty Images; 159: top AP/Bebeto Matthews, bottom © Peter Yates/Corbis; 162 © Chip East/Reuters/Corbis; 163 © Bettmann/ Corbis; 164 © Evan Schneider/ UN Photo/Zuma/Corbis; 165 © Reuters/Corbis; 166 Sukree Sukplang/Reuters/Landov; 167 © 2005 Jupiter Images Corporation (Shutterstock); 168 Permission courtesy of the City of Toronto Official Web Site/ Living in Toronto/Ecological Footprint (posted 2001) (www.toronto.ca/eia/footprint); 169 Reuters/Landov; 170 © Kevin Fleming/Corbis; 172 CP/New Brunswick Telegraph-Journal/Noel Chenier; 173 CP/Peterborough Examiner/Clifford Skarstedt; 174 Kyodo/Landov; 175 Christinne Muschi/Reuters/Landov; 176 © Reuters/Corbis; 177 UN/DPI photo by J. Isaac; 178 UN/DPI photo by M. Grant; 180 © Reuters/Corbis; 181 Farzana Wahidy/AFP/Getty Images; 182 NASA; 183 © Paul Vreeker/Reuters/Corbis; 184 © Bettmann/Corbis; 185 © David Turnley/Corbis; 186 © Patrick Robert/Sygma/Corbis; 187 © Langevin Jacques/Corbis Sygma; 188 © Jon Feingersh/Masterfile; 189 HotHouse Canada; 190 AP/Dennis Farrell; 191 Thony Belizaire/AFP/Getty Images; 192: left © Bogdan Cristel/Reuters/Corbis, centre © Charles Gupton/Corbis; 193 J.P. Moczulski/AFP/Getty Images; 194: top © 2005 Jupiter Images Corporation (Photos.com), bottom © 2005 Jupiter Images Corporation (ShutterStock); 195: right © Brownie Harris/Corbis, bottom © Ole Graf/Zefa/ Corbis; 196 Photodisc/Getty Images; 197: top © Jupiter Images Corporation (ShutterStock), centre © Chuck Savage/Corbis; 198 Photodisc/Getty Images; 199 © Tom Stewart/Corbis; 200 © John Henley/Corbis; 201 © Jupiter Images Corporation (ShutterStock); 202 © Jose Luis Pelaez, Inc./Corbis